Grandma's Classic Favorites

for
Holidays
and
Seasons

Grandma's Classic Favorites

for Holidays and Seasons

Kitchen Treasures by Paula Broberg

FRONT TABLE BOOKS

SPRINGVILLE, UTAH

© 2011 by Paula Broberg

ISBN: 978-1-59955-793-9

Published by Front Table Books, an imprint of Cedar Fort, Inc., 2373 W. 700 S., Springville, UT 84663
Distributed by Cedar Fort, Inc., www.cedarfort.com

LIBRARY OF CONGRESS CATALOGING-IN-PUBLICATION DATA
Broberg, Paula, 1943- author.
  Grandma's classic favorites for holidays and seasons / Paula Broberg.
      pages cm
   ISBN 978-1-59955-793-9
   1. Holiday cooking. I. Title.
   TX739.B76 2011
   641.5'68--dc22

      2011004033

Cover and page design by Megan Whittier
Cover design © 2011 by Lyle Mortimer
Edited by Megan E. Welton

Printed in China

10 9 8 7 6 5 4 3 2 1

Printed on acid-free paper

Contents

Introduction

These holiday celebrations share a common interest. They surround the enjoyable customs with the pleasures of tradition, which are meant to be shared with the family and friends you love. When people come together, memories are created.

Along with each menu, I will share with you ideas to enhance your holiday get-togethers, from gathering around a beautifully decorated table to sharing a delicious meal together, along with poems of the season. Celebrating the holidays gives us an opportunity to make our homes festive in the tradition of that month. It brings warmth and love into our homes as well as our hearts, creating an atmosphere that will radiate the spirit of each holiday with meaningful traditions and your loving touch.

The changes in our four seasons give us an opportunity to explore all the beauty of each one of them.

Spring is magic sweet to the senses——the sounds of the birds, the smell of the beautiful flowers, and the blossoms on the trees. We celebrate the rebirth of nature.

Summer is a fun and exciting season, full of enjoyment. The perennial flowers are in thick bloom. With the long, warm days and nights, gardens are in full swing, producing to abundance.

In the fall, there is a chill in the air, and the trees reflect nature's flaming colors with the changing of the season.

When winter approaches, the first snowfall has painted strokes of white across our once-green lawns. The days and nights are shorter now, and our weather turns colder while everything goes to sleep.

No matter what the holiday or season might be, cooking these recipes will bring sunshine home, all year long.

If Recipes Could Talk

If we recipes could talk, we would each have our own story to tell you about all the hundreds of times we've put smiles on someone's face, whether we were given as gifts, served up for a large group, prepared as a meal for two, or taken to the home of an ailing friend or family member to make them feel better. Maybe we were even baked up for a party or whipped up for an after-school snack.

We have traveled several thousands of miles through the years and have been passed around to so many people; now we live on in homes all over, where we are loved and thought of as being a piece of comfort and joy. And we are never spoken of without someone mentioning how much we are loved.

Each of us offers a legacy: some of us are youngsters just starting out and haven't been around for long. Others of us have stood the test of time and have always come out valiant. A few of us date back to the 1800s, eight generations previous. But our age doesn't matter—we are just as good as the day we were created.

And now we're being given to you. We hope you will love us and take good care of us. Set us in a perfect spot—a safe place in your kitchen. Keep us clean and spotless, and each time you look at us, consider us to be your Kitchen Treasures.

So cook us up and show us off. Let your family and friends see how wonderful we are, because we want to see smiles on faces and cause warmth in hearts, not to mention fill up tummies like we have done for the last two hundred years.

We were given to you because you are so special—one of a kind, just like us. I hope you will enjoy us as much as we will enjoy being with you from now on. And one day you will have someone special—a daughter or son you will pass us on to, and they will love us too. This is our gift to you from Grandma's kitchen.

—Paula Broberg

New Year's Day

'A Resolution for New Beginnings"

New Year's Day is a day many people like to stay in bed a little longer in the morning, especially if they were out **celebrating** New Year's Eve the night before. Maybe you start the day a little slower by turning on the television and waking up to the **Pasadena Rose Parade** with all the beautiful floats. Maybe in the afternoon, you invite some friends or family over to watch some **football,** serving up some dips and other yummy snack foods to munch on. And after the games are over, here is a quick, easy, make-ahead menu that's sure to please whatever crowd you have.

Menu

Sausage Cheese Balls

This is a great treat to make ahead. Either cook them immediately, keep them in the refrigerator overnight, or freeze them!

Ingredients

- 1 lb. lean pork hot sausage
- 3 cups baking mix
- ½ lb. sharp cheese, grated

Directions

If baking immediately, preheat oven to 400 degrees.

Allow ingredients to reach room temperature. Combine sausage, baking mix, and cheese thoroughly and form into small balls. To freeze, arrange sausage balls on a cookie sheet and freeze individually, then transfer into freezer-safe bags. When you're ready to serve, thaw sausage—about 15 minutes—and bake for 15 minutes at 400 degrees.

Creamy Herb Dip

This is delicious on fresh veggies!

Ingredients

- 4 oz. cream cheese, softened
- ¼ cup buttermilk
- 1 Tbsp. fresh parsley, minced
- 1 tsp. dried dill
- 2 Tbsp. chives, minced
- ¼ tsp. kosher salt
- 1 tsp. lemon rind, grated
- 1 garlic clove, minced
- ⅛ tsp. fresh ground pepper
- 1 large red pepper (for use as serving bowl)

Serve With

- 1 cup broccoli pieces
- 1 cup cauliflower pieces
- 1 cup baby carrots
- 1 cup jicama
- 2 stalks celery, cut into 3-inch sticks
- 1 red pepper, sliced

Directions

In a blender, combine all ingredients and blend until smooth. Cut off the top of large red pepper approximately 1 to 1½ inches down from stem. Scoop out seeds and core. Rinse in cold water and dry with paper towel. Place hollowed pepper in the center of a large platter to serve as the bowl. Spoon herb dip into pepper bowl, and arrange vegetables around it for dipping.

Paula Broberg

Artichoke Dip

If you plan on having a few friends over and you need a quick, easy, and delicious dish to serve to start off your evening, this one it will be a hit.

Ingredients

- 2 (6-oz.) jars marinated artichoke hearts, chopped
- 1 Tbsp. garlic powder
- ¾ cup mayonnaise
- 1 cup Parmesan cheese
- Dash Tabasco sauce
- French bread slices, warmed

Directions

Preheat oven to 350 degrees.

Combine all ingredients in a medium mixing bowl. Pour into a 9x9-inch baking dish and bake for 20 minutes. Remove from oven and scoop into a serving bowl placed in the center of a platter of hot French bread slices. Spread dip over bread and enjoy!

New Year's Day

Welsh's Famous Chili

This is a recipe from my good friend Jim Welsh. There are many ways to make chili, and I have tried a lot of them, but this hot and hearty chili is my favorite. One dish makes two different meals!

Ingredients

- 3 lbs. ground beef
- 1 onion, chopped
- 1 Tbsp. chili powder, or to taste
- 2 (15.5-oz.) cans chili beans
- 2 (14.5-oz.) cans stewed tomatoes
- 2 (15-oz.) cans tomato sauce
- 1 (27-oz.) can whole green chilies
- 1 cup mild cheddar cheese, shredded (optional)

Directions

In a large cast iron skillet, brown ground beef, onions, and chili powder until beef is cooked through. Transfer beef and onion mixture into a large soup pot. Add chili beans, tomatoes, tomato sauce, and green chilies to beef and onion mixture. Bring to a boil, then reduce heat to a simmer. Cook, covered, approximately 30 to 45 minutes. Serve hot and top with cheese, if desired.

For Chili Spaghetti

Ingredients

- 1 lb. vermicelli or spaghetti
- Chili, see above
- 1 onion, chopped
- 1 cup mild cheddar cheese, shredded

Directions

Prepare vermicelli or spaghetti according to package directions. Drain. Place cooked pasta in large bowl and pour hot chili over top. Add chopped onion and shredded cheese and serve.

Paula Broberg

Honey Corn Bread

Ingredients

- 1 box corn bread muffin mix
- ⅔ cups milk
- 1 egg
- ⅓ cup butter melted
- 1 Tbsp. honey
- ½ cup shredded cheddar cheese (optional)
- 1 (14.25-oz.) can creamed corn (optional)
- ¼ cup chopped green onions (optional)
- 1 (4-oz.) can diced green chilies (optional)

Directions

Preheat oven to 400 degrees, and lightly grease a 9x9-inch baking pan or spray with nonstick cooking spray.

In a large mixing bowl, add the first five ingredients and stir until moistened. Add any other optional ingredients if desired. Spoon batter into prepared pan and bake until golden brown, 22–26 minutes.

New Year's Day

Valentine's Day

"A Celebration of Love"

There are several different stories about a man named **Valentine,** a priest who served during the third century in Rome. Legend has it that Valentine himself actually sent the first "Valentine Card" to a young girl he fell in **love** with, which he signed, "From Your Valentine." Now, every February, children and adults all across the nation enjoy sending cards, candy, and flowers to the ones they love. When you think of Valentine's Day, you think of love and **romance.** It's a celebration of the senses. Things that taste, smell, feel, sound, and look beautiful is what romance is all about. If you want an especially romantic time, try to appeal to all the senses, and use your imagination.

Menu

Spinach Pecan Salad

Ingredients

- 1 (5-oz.) package baby spinach, washed
- 1 cup cherry or grape tomatoes
- 1 avocado, diced
- 1 cup dried cranberries
- 1 cup pecan, nuts whole or chopped
- ½ cup feta cheese

Directions

Place spinach in the bottom of a serving bowl. Arrange tomatoes around the edge of the bowl. Arrange avocado in a circle within the tomatoes. Repeat with cranberries, pecans, and feta cheese so there's a nested circle of each, like a target. Cover with plastic wrap and refrigerate until ready to serve. Add your favorite dressing right before serving.

"The best way to stay young at heart is to love."

Valentine's Day

Lobster Tail

serves 2

Ingredients

- 2 (½-pound) lobster tails
- 2 Tbsp. butter, melted
- 2 tsp. lemon juice
- Paprika

Directions

Preheat broiler to 400 degrees.

With kitchen shears, cut down the top of the shell until you reach the fin. Gently pry apart the meat with thumbs. Starting from the fin end, use thumbs to separate meat from shell. Pour melted butter over top and sprinkle with lemon juice and paprika. Broil for 25 minutes. Make sure not to overcook, or lobster meat will get tough. Serve hot with melted butter for dipping.

Twice Baked Twice Loved Potatoes

When you try a forkful of these potatoes, your mouth will think you've gone to heaven. A perfect complement to any special dinner.

serves 4

Ingredients

- 4 medium baking potatoes
- 4 Tbsp. butter, softened, + 2 Tbsp. melted butter for potato skins
- 4 Tbsp. sour cream
- 2 oz. cream cheese
- 2 Tbsp. half and half
- 4 Tbsp. Velveeta cheese
- Sea salt and pepper to taste
- 2 stalks green onion, chopped
- 2 strips bacon, cooked till crisp and crumbled
- ½ cup cheddar cheese, grated

Directions

Preheat oven to 325 degrees and line a cookie sheet with foil.

Prick potatoes with fork before baking to allow excess steam to escape. Brush skins with melted butter and arrange potatoes on foil-lined cookie sheet. Bake for approximately 1 hour or until a fork pierces potato easily. Remove from oven. When just cool enough to handle, cut potatoes lengthwise, scoop out potatoes, leaving skins as much intact as possible.

In a large bowl, combine potato with butter, sour cream, cream cheese, half and half, Velveeta, and salt and pepper to taste. Mix together with an electric mixer until creamy. Stuff skins with potato mixture and top with cheddar cheese. Return to oven and bake for an additional 15 minutes. Serve hot from the oven, topped with green onions and bacon.

Peach Glazed Carrots

"Love is like having caviar for an appetizer, filet mignon for an entrée, and crepe Suzette for dessert."

Ingredients

- 1 lb. baby carrots
- ½ cup peach preserves
- 1 Tbsp. butter, softened
- 2 Tbsp. brown sugar

Directions

Preheat oven to 350 degrees.

Arrange carrots in a 9x9-inch baking dish. In a small bowl, combine peach preserves, butter, and brown sugar. Spoon mixture over carrots. Bake for approximately 5 minutes, or until carrots are tender.

twice baked potatoes

Valentine's Day

New York Cheesecake

Bake this creamy creation in a spring form pan so the cake will unmold neatly. This gorgeously rich cake is best served in 12 to 16 small wedges.

Crumb Crust

Ingredients

- 1½ cups graham cracker crumbs
- ¼ cup sugar
- ½ cup (1 cube) butter, melted

Directions

Combine graham cracker crumbs and sugar in a medium bowl. Blend in melted butter. In a 9-inch buttered spring form pan, press graham cracker mixture firmly across the bottom and about 2½ inches up the sides. Chill.

Filling directions continued on page 18

Valentine's Day

Filling for New York Cheesecake

Ingredients

- 3 (8-oz.) packages cream cheese, softened
- 1¼ cups sugar
- ⅛ tsp. salt
- 3 eggs
- 1 tsp. vanilla
- 2 cups sour cream

Topping

- 2 cups sour cream
- ½ cup sugar
- ¼ tsp. vanilla
- 1 cup sliced strawberries, for garnish (optional)

Directions

Preheat oven to 350 degrees.

Let cream cheese soften in large bowl until room temperature. Blend in 1¼ cups sugar and salt and beat until fluffy. Add eggs one at a time, beating well after each addition. Add in 1 tsp. vanilla and mix well.

Pour cream cheese mixture into crumb crust. Bake for 50 minutes or until firm in center. Remove cake from oven, let stand 15 minutes and reset oven to 450 degrees.

In a medium bowl, mix together topping ingredients. Spread sour cream mixture over top of cake and return to oven for 10 minutes or until topping is set. Cool cake on wire rack and chill completely. Loosen cake around edges with knife. Release spring and remove sides of pan, leaving cake on metal base for easy handling and serving. For a party, touch up top with a rosette of sliced strawberries.

St. Patrick's Day

"An Irish Holiday Tradition"

St. Patrick was the patron saint of Ireland. St. Patrick died at Soul Downpatrick, Ireland on March 17, 460 AD. The first recorded St. Patrick's Day celebration outside of Ireland was at Parliament in Westminster in 1719. In 1900, Queen Victoria ordered shamrocks to be worn by the Irish soldiers on St. Patrick's Day in memory of their fellow Irishmen. Now, St. Patrick is the focal point of Dublin's annual festival that includes fireworks, exhibitions, music, dancing, and a parade. This is a day every year Ireland and many other parts of the world celebrate their Irishness. The shamrock is still very much associated with St. Patrick and is traditionally worn on Saint Patrick's Day. It is also Ireland's national emblem. The shamrock is considered a good luck symbol by many people worldwide.

Menu

Split Pea Soup

serves 4 to 6

Ingredients

- 2 cups split peas
- 6 to 8 cups cold water
- 2 quarts organic chicken broth
- 2 ham hocks or 2 cups diced ham
- 1 clove garlic, minced
- ¾ cup celery diced with leaves
- 1 cup sliced baby carrots
- 1 medium onion, chopped
- 1 bay leaf
- Sea salt and fresh ground pepper to taste
- 2 Tbsp. milk

Directions

Rinse and sort peas in large pot. Add 6-8 cups cold water. Let stand overnight or for at least 6-8 hours. Drain off water and rinse peas. In same pot, pour in chicken broth, add soaked peas, ham, garlic, celery, carrots, onion, and bay leaf. Simmer for 2 to 3 hours, stirring occasionally. Season with salt and pepper to taste. When ready to eat, remove bay leaf and add milk. Remove soup from heat and pour into a large, warmed tureen or individual soup bowls and serve immediately.

Avocado Lime Jell-O

This is a Jell-O salad is my husband Ken's favorite. His mother, Edna, always made it for him. In fact, she didn't want to share her recipes, because then she wouldn't have something special to serve when he would come home for dinner. As it turns out, I got all her recipes years later, and he is still enjoying them today.

Ingredients

- 1 box lime Jell-O
- 1 cup boiling water
- 4 Tbsp. lemon juice
- 1 tsp. salt
- 1 (20-oz.) can pineapple crushed, with juice
- 1 cup avocado, diced
- 1 cup mayonnaise
- ½ pint heavy whipping cream, whipped

Directions

In medium mixing bowl, dissolve Jell-O in boiling water, add lemon juice, salt, pineapple and the juice. Stir well, then refrigerate until partially set up, about 30 minutes.

In a medium bowl, mix together avacado, mayonnaise, and whipped cream. Combine avocado mixture with partially set Jell-O. Pour into a 9x13-inch glass dish or into individual serving glasses for more holiday elegance.

Corned Beef and Cabbage

Ingredients

- 1 (3-lb.) corned beef brisket
- 2 tsp. pickling spice
- 6 carrots, cut into 3-inch pieces
- 6 red potatoes, cut in half
- 1 large onion, peeled and quartered
- 1 head cabbage, quartered
- 1 tsp. sugar
- 2 Tbsp. butter, melted
- Fresh chopped parsley, for garnish

Directions

Wipe corned beef with damp paper towels. Place in large stockpot, cover with water, and add pickling spices. Bring to a boil, reduce heat, and simmer for 5 minutes. Skim excess fat from surface. Simmer brisket, covered, for 3 to 4 more hours or until fork tender. Add carrots, potatoes, and onion in last 25 minutes. Add cabbage during last 15 minutes and sprinkle sugar over cabbage. Continue to cook until vegetables are just tender.

Slice corned beef across grain, and arrange slices on platter with vegetables. Brush potatoes with butter, and sprinkle with chopped parsley.

Irish Soda Bread

Sweet, crusty, and made without yeast, Irish soda bread is a real treat. Baking soda and buttermilk are the key ingredients, but the real trick lies in the baking, especially in the cast iron "pot oven," or "Dutch oven," as it's known in America.

Ingredients

- 1 Tbsp. butter
- 4 cups white bread flour
- 1 tsp. salt
- 1 tsp. baking soda
- 1 cup buttermilk

Directions

Preheat oven to 375 degrees.

Cut the butter into the flour until the combination reaches a fine crumb texture. Add salt and baking soda and run mixture through your fingers until will combined. Add buttermilk and mix into a soft dough. Turn out dough onto a lightly floured surface and knead about 3 minutes until smooth. Shape into a round about 2 inches thick and fit into well-greased pot oven. Using a sharp knife dipped in flour, mark a cross a ½ inch deep in the dough—known as farls or quarters in Irish—then bake for 40 minutes. Thump the bottom of loaf to test for doneness. If it sounds hollow, it's done!

Pistachio Pecan Cake

Ingredients

- 1 box white cake mix
- ¾ cup oil
- 3 eggs
- 1 cup lemon-lime or club soda
- 8 oz. sour cream
- 1 (4-oz.) package instant pistachio pudding
- 1 cup pecans, chopped
- ½ cup coconut, shredded

"It would be better to live in a small little cottage where there is love than in a large palace where there are just tears."

Directions

Preheat oven to 350 degrees, and spray a bundt pan with cooking spray.

In a large bowl and using an electric mixer, combine cake mix, oil, eggs, soda, sour cream and pudding mix, until creamy. Fold in pecans and coconut.

Pour batter into prepared bundt pan and bake for 35 to 45 minutes or until a toothpick inserted in cake comes out clean. Allow cake to cool on a wire rack. Invert cake onto a plate to serve.

Paula Broberg

Easter

"A Celebration of Joy"

The first Easter was well established by the second century. In 325 A.D., the council of Nicaea established the tradition of celebrating **Easter** on the first Sunday to occur after the first full moon on or after the vernal equinox, which is between the dates of March 22 and April 25. Easter is the day when Christians observe the resurrection of **Jesus Christ.** On the third day of his crucifixion, Jesus Christ became the first person to be resurrected. His body and spirit were reunited, never to be separated again. Easter celebrations involve a lot of symbolism. The **egg** has always been a symbol of new life, and it's oval shape is equated with infinity...no beginning, no end. Giving eggs to one another at this season is believed, in some cultures, to be a sign of good luck in the new year. Coloring eggs in the spring is a very old custom dating back thousands of years to ancient Egyptians, Persians, and Chinese. Swiss children receive in their eggs a bird, the Easter cuckoo. The more common **Easter bunny** tradition comes from a German fable, where the rabbit brought eggs to the good children.

Menu

Waldorf Salad

Ingredients

- 1 cup apples
- 1 cup peeled oranges
- 1 cup celery
- ½ cup raisins
- 1 cup walnuts
- ½ cup whipping cream
- ½ cup mayonnaise

Directions

Cut fruit and vegetables into bite-sized pieces, and combine with raisins and nuts in a large bowl. In a separate bowl, mix together whipping cream and mayonnaise. Pour mayonnaise mixture over fruit and mix well. Refrigerate and serve chilled.

Easter

Yeast Rolls

This is a recipe my niece Paula Krejci gave me. She uses it to make her family rolls, pizza dough, cinnamon rolls, and more.

Ingredients

- 2½ cups warm water
- 5 tsp. quick yeast
- 1 Tbsp. salt
- 1 Tbsp. sugar
- 5 to 7 cups flour

Directions

Preheat oven to 375 degrees.

Mix all ingredients except flour in a large bowl. Gradually add flour until dough is no longer sticky. Knead for about 10 minutes on floured bread board. Roll dough out into circle about 1 inch thick. Cut into biscuit-size pieces about 2 inches in diameter. Arrange rolls on a cookie sheet about 2 inches apart. Bake for 20 to 25 minutes or until lightly brown.

Easter

Grandma's Classic Favorites for Holidays and Seasons

Asparagus with Cream Sauce

Ingredients

- 1½ lbs. fresh asparagus
- ½ cup heavy cream
- ¼ cup white wine
- 1 tsp. Dijon mustard
- 3 Tbsp. butter

Directions

Steam asparagus until tender crisp. Combine cream, wine, and mustard in a small saucepan and cook over medium-high heat, stirring constantly until sauce is reduced by half. Reduce heat and stir in butter until melted. Arrange asparagus on a serving plate and pour sauce over top.

"It's not the momentary satisfaction of what we want, or think we need, that fulfills our lives, but the realization and showing of gratitude for how much we already have been blessed with."

Paula Broberg

Scalloped Potatoes

Ingredients

- 8 small potatoes, peeled
- 1 small onion
- 2 cups milk
- 3 Tbsp. flour
- 2 Tbsp. butter
- Salt and pepper
- 4 oz. Velveeta cheese
- 2 oz. medium parsley flakes
- 1 cup grated cheddar cheese

Directions

Preheat oven to 350 degrees.

Thinly slice potatoes and onion. Cook together in boiling water until just before done Drain and arrange in a 9x13-inch baking dish. Combine milk and flour in a medium saucepan and heat over medium until slightly thickened and add butter. Season with salt and pepper to taste. Add Velveeta cheese and cook until melted. Pour sauce over potatoes, and sprinkle grated cheddar cheese and parsley over top. Bake potatoes for 25 minutes or until cheese starts bubbling.

Easter

Mimi's Carrot Cake

I like to serve this moist, melt-in-your-mouth cake at Easter. But since it's a favorite in our family, we serve it up much more often than that. I'm sure it will be a favorite of yours too.

Ingredients

- 1½ cups oil
- 2 cups sugar
- 3 eggs
- 2 cups + 4 Tbsp. flour
- 1 tsp. salt
- 2 tsp. baking soda
- 2 tsp. baking powder
- 2 tsp. cinnamon
- 3 cups carrots grated
- 1 cup walnuts chopped

Frosting

- ½ cup (1 cube) butter, softened
- 1 (8-oz.) package cream cheese, softened
- 1 tsp. vanilla
- 1 (16-oz.) package powdered sugar

Directions on page 32

Easter

Directions for Mimi's Carrot Cake

Preheat oven to 350 degrees.

In a large mixing bowl, beat together oil and sugar with an electric mixer until smooth. Add eggs and continue to beat until smooth and creamy. In separate bowl, sift flour, salt, baking soda, baking powder, and cinnamon together. Gradually add flour mixture to cream mixture, stirring just until mixed. Stir in carrots and walnuts. Bake for 35 minutes or until a toothpick inserted into the center of cake comes out clean. Allow cake to cool before frosting.

While cake is cooling, make frosting. With an electric mixer, combine butter, cream cheese, and vanilla until smooth. Gradually add powdered sugar, beating with electric mixer until smooth.

Ham with Plum Sauce

This is a delicious way to prepare a holiday ham.

Ingredients

- 1 (8-oz.) can crushed pineapple with juice
- ⅓ (8-oz.) bottle plum sauce
- 1 cup brown sugar
- ½ tsp. mustard powder
- 1 ham

Directions

Combine all ingredients except ham in a medium saucepan and cook over low heat for approximately 10 minutes. Pour half of plum mixture over ham and bake according to instructions on ham. When serving, pour the remaining sauce into a small dish to serve along side of ham.

Easter

ham with plum sauce, p. 33

Mother's Day

"A Tribute to Motherhood"

The first Mother's Day was observed in 1907 in Philadelphia based on suggestions given by Julia Howe in 1872, along with Anna Jarvis in the year 1907. Mother's Day is a time when children make handmade cards, **give flowers,** and make long distance calls to those too far away to spend the day or share in the celebration. Mother's Day is a day we honor motherhood and set it apart on the second Sunday in May of each year. Many churches make that day special for **mothers** by giving talks to honor them and all they do. For a perfect high tea party, enjoy the fun and satisfaction that comes from creating a beautiful setting. Use your lace tablecloth, your finest antique china dishes, and a centerpiece of fresh cut flowers. Serve fresh seasonal fruit to complement your menu. Create a day to remember, not only for your own mother, but also for **grandmothers** or anyone else who comes who is a mother. Make them feel special on this day. Consider placing a long stem rose tied with ribbon where each guest will sit. Honor your mother with a gift, by reading a poem to her, or sharing a childhood experience with your guests.

Menu

Broccoli Cheese Soup

Ingredients

- 1 large head broccoli
- 2 cups chicken broth
- ¼ cup butter (½ cube)
- 1 small onion, minced
- ¼ cup carrots, grated
- 1 garlic clove, minced
- ½ cup celery, minced, plus tops
- 2 cups milk
- 1 cup half and half
- 1 cup cheddar cheese, grated

Roux

- 4 Tbsp. butter
- 4 Tbsp. flour

Directions

Trim broccoli and cut into small florets. In a soup pot, cook broccoli in chicken broth until tender. In a large skillet, melt butter and sauté onions, carrots, garlic, and celery. Combine sautéed vegetables and cooked broccoli in a blender or food processor and process until partly smooth. Pour processed mixture back into soup pot and add milk and half and half.

In the same skillet used to sauté vegetables, melt butter over medium heat and stir in flour to make a roux. Cook for 2 to 3 minutes until bubbly and lightly brown. Add to soup mixture while stirring constantly. Stir soup until it reaches a light boil, reduce heat, simmer. Add salt and pepper to taste. Ladle into hot bowls, and top with cheddar cheese.

Paula Broberg

Mother's Day

Cashew Chicken Salad

serves 10 to 15

This salad is especially good, just like the person who created it. My Aunt Jane served it a lot at her church dinners.

Ingredients

- 2 cups macaroni, cooked
- 1½ cups cashews
- 1 Tbsp. chopped onion
- 6 to 7 cups cooked chicken breast
- 1 large can of pineapple chunks, with juice
- 1 to 2 cups diced golden delicious apples
- 2 cups chopped celery
- 2 cups whole green grapes
- 2 cups water chestnuts, chopped

Dressing

- 1 cup mayonnaise
- 1 cup of Hidden Valley ranch dressing

Directions

Combine all ingredients in a large serving bowl. In a separate bowl, mix together dressing ingredients and pour over top of chicken salad. Mix well. Refrigerate until ready to serve.

broccoli cheese soup

Raspberry Tea

Ingredients

- 1 pot fresh brewed raspberry herbal tea
- 1 cup fresh raspberries smashed
- ¼ cup raspberries whole
- 1 tsp. honey per cup

Directions

Brew tea according to package directions. Stir in smashed raspberries and set aside for a few minutes, allowing tea to pick up the additional flavor. Pour tea into cups and stir in honey. Top each cup of tea with 2 or 3 raspberries each.

Mother's Day

Paula Broberg

Berry Trifle Fit for a Queen

serves 6 to 8

A trifle is a wonderful English dessert perfect for tea.

Ingredients

- 1 (3.4-oz.) package vanilla instant pudding, prepared
- 3 cups fresh blackberries, sweetened to taste
- 1 (5x9-inch) pound cake, homemade or store-bought, sliced
- 2 cups whipped cream

Directions

Prepare vanilla pudding according to package directions.

In a parfait glass, layer ingredients in the following order: sweetened blackberries, a slice of pound cake, pudding, and whipped cream. Repeat layers and top with a couple of blackberries. Repeat with remaining parfait glasses.

Mother's Day

Famous English Scones

Ingredients

- 4 cups flour
- 1 cup sugar
- 1½ tsp. baking soda
- 3 tsp. cream of tartar
- ¼ tsp. salt
- 1 cup unsalted butter (2 cubes), softened
- 1 cup dried cranberries
- ½ cup buttermilk
- 2 eggs, beaten
- ½ cup roasted almond pieces (optional)

Directions

Preheat oven to 350 degrees.

In a large bowl, run flour, sugar, baking soda, cream of tarter, and salt through a sifter twice. Using a pastry blender, cut in butter until it reaches a coarse grain texture. Stir in cranberries. In a separate bowl, combine buttermilk and beaten eggs. Add buttermilk-egg mixture to form a stiff dough. On a floured surface, roll out dough in a round 1½ inches thick. Cut scones using a 2-inch biscuit cutter. Place scones on a lined and greased lined baking sheet. Bake until golden brown.

Serve with whipped cream and your favorite preserves or lemon curd (see page 108).

Mother's Day

Father's Day

"A Tribute to Fatherhood"

The first Father's Day celebration was held in Spokane, Washington on June 19, 1910. A woman by the name of Sonora Smart thought that there should be a special day to **honor fathers.** In 1924, President Calvin Coolidge officially proclaimed the third Sunday in June as Father's Day. Father's Day is a day to celebrate fathers, stepfathers, grandfathers, and uncles—any man who's supported you in your life. A father is someone who is **patient,** loving, and kind. He is someone who listens when you have something on your mind. He is proud of your accomplishments. And each year that passes, you're even more glad and **proud** to call him Dad. A father's love plays a part in all you do, and he will always hold a special place for you deep within his heart.

Menu

Strawberry Pecan Salad

Ingredients

- 1 (5-oz.) bag spring salad mix
- 1 pint fresh sliced strawberries
- 1 cup feta cheese crumbs
- 1 cup pecan halves

Dressing

- ⅔ cups olive oil
- 3 Tbsp. raspberry vinegar
- 1 Tbsp. sugar
- 1 clove garlic peeled, crushed
- Salt and pepper to taste

Directions

Whisk together olive oil, raspberry vinegar, sugar, and garlic, or shake ingredients together in a jar. Add salt and pepper to taste. In a large serving bowl, arrange spring mix, strawberries, feta cheese, and pecan halves. Just before serving, toss salad with dressing.

Ken's Barbecue Chicken and Ribs

My husband has perfected this truly delicious honey barbecue sauce. It was always just "a pinch of this and a dash of that." But he was finally nice enough to write down the exact measurements when I was ready to get this book published.

Ingredients

- 1 (18-oz.) bottle honey barbecue sauce
- ½ cup ketchup
- 1 Tbsp. Tabasco sauce
- 1 Tbsp. garlic powder
- 1 Tbsp. lemon pepper
- 1 Tbsp. soy sauce
- 1 Tbsp. Worcestershire sauce
- 2 Tbsp. parsley
- 2 Tbsp. Molly McButter
- 1½ tsp. seasoning salt
- ½ cup brown sugar
- ½ cup honey
- ¼ cup water
- 1 large rack pork ribs
- 1 lb. chicken pieces

Directions

Preheat oven to 300 degrees.

Preheat grill to medium-high heat.

Bake chicken and ribs in separate baking dishes for approximately 1½ hours or until tender. While meat is roasting, combine all sauce ingredients in a bowl and mix thoroughly. Place roasted meat on heated grill, basting each side with prepared sauce. Cook each side for about 3 minutes until nice grill lines form, but be sure not to let meat burn.

Potato Casserole

Ingredients

- 1 (24-oz.) package country style frozen hash browns
- 1 (10.75-oz.) can cream of chicken soup
- ⅓ cup green onions, chopped
- 1 cup sour cream
- 2 cups cheddar cheese, grated
- ¼ cup melted butter (½ cube)
- 1 cup corn flakes crumbs

Directions

Preheat oven to 300 degrees.

Thaw and drain hash browns. In a medium bowl, mix soup, onions, sour cream, cheese, and butter. Add hash browns to soup mixture and combine thoroughly. Pour into buttered baking pan or casserole dish. Sprinkle top of casserole evenly with corn flake crumbs. Bake until bubbly, approximately 30 minutes.

Fresh Green Beans

Ingredients

- 1 bunch celery, chopped into large chunks
- 3 bell peppers, chopped into large chunks
- 3 small onions, chopped
- 3 sprigs fresh parsley, chopped
- ¼ cup olive oil
- ½ cup butter (1 cube)
- 1 lb. mushrooms, quartered
- ½ lb. bacon, cooked and diced
- 3 lbs. fresh green beans
- Salt and pepper to taste

Directions

In a large skillet, sauté celery, green peppers, onions, and parsley in olive oil and butter. Cover and cook vegetables until tender, about 3 minutes, then add mushrooms and crisp fried bacon. In a large pot over medium heat, combine green beans and sautéed vegetables. Cover and cook until green beans are tender.

Add salt and pepper to taste

fresh green beans

Garlic Bread

Ingredients

- 1 whole head fresh garlic cloves, chopped
- ½ cup butter (1 cube), sliced
- 1 loaf French bread
- 4 oz. fresh Parmesan cheese
- 4 sprigs fresh parsley, chopped

Directions

Preheat broiler to 450 degrees.

Sauté garlic in butter until lightly brown. Slice French bread into ¼-inch slices and arrange on a baking sheet. Brush sautéed garlic onto bread slices. Grate cheese over bread and sprinkle with parsley. Set bread under broiler until cheese bubbles and turns light brown.

banana cream pie, p. 48

Banana Cream Pie

This is the best banana cream pie I have ever had. My thanks goes to Bev Layer for this recipe. Bev, I have made this many times, and it is always a hit.

Ingredients

- 1 cup powdered sugar
- 8 oz. cream cheese, softened
- 1 pint whipped cream
- 1 baked pie crust (see recipe on page 64)
- 1 (3.4-oz.) box instant vanilla pudding
- 1¼ cups milk
- 5 to 6 medium bananas

> "A father is someone who used to watch the Super Bowl on TV, but who now goes to Pop Warner football games and watches his son, the future football star."

Directions

Beat powdered sugar, cream cheese, and 1 cup whipped cream until smooth and spread into pie crust. Chill in refrigerator. Beat pudding and milk together in a small bowl for 2 to 3 minutes or until thick and set aside. Slice bananas and arrange in an even layer over cream cheese mixture. Top bananas with vanilla pudding mixture. Spread remaining whipped cream over pudding and refrigerate until ready to serve.

Independence Day

"The Spirit of America and Freedom"

The Fourth of July is special to Americans. It was on this date in 1776 that the original thirteen colonies celebrated their **independence** from England. Now we celebrate this grand holiday in a variety of ways: parades, **fireworks,** bonfires, picnics, and barbecues. It's a time for families and friends to gather together for a wonderful time. We go to lakes, mountains, beaches, parks, and backyards. Wherever we go, we enjoy the festivities of **patriotism.** As **Americans,** we fly our flags of red, white, and blue, originally designed by Betsy Ross with stars and stripes. People today decorate their homes with tablecloths, plates, napkins, centerpieces, and flowers, all in **red, white, and blue,** in tribute to our wonderful country.

Menu

Paula's Kentucky Fried Chicken

Because I was born in Kentucky, being able to cook a delicious fried chicken dinner, complete with mashed potatoes, biscuits, and gravy was a necessity. My grandmother made this every Sunday for all of her children and grandchildren.

Ingredients

- 1 whole chicken, cut up
- ½ cup flour
- ½ cup baking mix
- Salt and pepper to taste
- ½ to ¾ cup olive oil
- Lawry's Seasoned Salt
- ¼ cube butter

> "Proclaim liberty throughout the land unto all the inhabitants thereof."
> —Inscription on the Liberty Bell

Directions

Wash cut up chicken and pat dry with paper towels. Mix flour and baking mix together. Coat both sides of chicken and set aside on a plate. Sprinkle one side of chicken with salt and pepper. Heat olive oil in a cast iron skillet over medium high heat. Place chicken into rippling oil, salt and pepper side down. Sprinkle seasoned salt and pepper over chicken. Cook, covered, over medium heat until light golden brown. Turn chicken and brown other side. Add small pats of butter around chicken and cook with lid partly on. Total cooking time is approximately 45 minutes. Cook chicken until juices run clear and the chicken is firm but tender. It should be golden brown all over. Remove chicken from skillet and drain on paper towels.

Mom's Potato Salad

This is a recipe that my mother would always
serve for picnics or backyard barbecues.

Ingredients

- 8 medium potatoes, diced
- 6 hard boiled eggs, chopped
- 2 stalks celery, chopped
- 1 medium onion, chopped
- 1 cup mayonnaise
- 1 Tbsp. sweet pickle relish
- 1 Tbsp. sweet pickle juice
- 1 Tbsp. Dijon mustard
- 1 sprig parsley
- Salt and pepper to taste
- Paprika

"War is not love, war is not peace,
war is not right—this is the lesson that
we teach. To people of the world who
were caused sorrow and pain, solders
have given their lives that we might
gain freedom and victory with out
shame. War is not fair; war is not fair.
—Jaime Troughton, Granddaughter

Directions

Scrub potatoes and place in large pot of boiling water. Cover and cook until tender. Set
aside until cool, then cut into bite-size cubes. In a large serving bowl, mix, celery, onion,
eggs, and cubed potatoes and set aside. In a small bowl, mix mayonnaise, pickle relish,
pickle juice, and mustard. Add mayonnaise mixture to other ingredients. Add salt and
pepper to taste and extra mayonnaise if necessary. Garnish with parsley sprigs and
lightly sprinkle paprika over top. Refrigerate for 2 to 3 hours or until ready to serve.

Independence Day

Broccoli Salad

I love making this dish as a side salad for summer suppers.

Ingredients

- 2 large bunches broccoli, cut into florets
- ½ cup slivered almonds
- 1 red onion, diced
- 5 slices bacon, cooked and diced
- ½ cup dried cranberries
- ½ cup white vinegar
- ½ cup sugar
- 1 cup mayonnaise

Directions

In a large mixing bowl, combine broccoli, almonds, onion, bacon, and cranberries and set aside. Boil together vinegar and sugar in saucepan until sugar is dissolved. Remove from heat and let cool. Add mayonnaise to vinegar mixture and whip till creamy. Add dressing to broccoli mix and toss until evenly distributed. Chill salad until ready to serve.

Fresh Fruit Salad

Ingredients

- 1 cup strawberries, halved
- 1 cup blueberries, whole
- 1 cup apples, peeled and diced
- 1 cup green grapes, whole
- 1 cup oranges, peeled and sliced
- 1 cup walnuts, quartered
- 1 cup fresh pineapple bits
- 1 cup bananas, sliced
- 1 cup strawberry or peach yogurt
- 1 cup mayonnaise

Directions

In a large bowl, mix together berries and fruit and chill in refrigerator. In a separate bowl, mix together yogurt and mayonnaise. Add to chilled fruit and toss to distribute evenly.

stars and stripes flag cake, p. 56

Stars and Stripes Flag Cake

This is a recipe that one of our friends
brought to our Fourth of July picnic one year.

Ingredients

- 1 box white cake mix
- 1 cup heavy cream
- 1 Tbsp. sugar
- ½ tsp. vanilla
- ½ cup fresh blueberries
- 2 cups fresh strawberries, sliced

> "It's an honor to make peace
> in this country of ours."
> —Kenneth Broberg

Directions

Bake cake according to package directions in a 9x13-inch baking pan. Place cake on attractive serving dish or platter. Beat cream until soft peaks form. Add sugar and vanilla. Spread whipped cream in an even layer over top of cake. Place two lines of blueberries at right angles in top left corner to form a 4-inch square. Fill square with additional lines of blueberries. Leave small amount of white cream showing between the berries. Think white stars on the American Flag. Using strawberry slices, form horizontal red stripes from side to side on cake, allowing cream to show for white stripes. Refrigerate cake until serving time.

Variation: Bake cake batter into small cupcakes and top with whipped cream, blueberries and strawberries.

Labor Day

"The Working Man's Holiday"

The first Labor Day was celebrated on Tuesday, September 5, 1882, in New York City. In 1884, the city decided to celebrate the "Working Man's Holiday" annually on the first Monday in September. It wasn't until ten years later, in 1894, that Congress passed a law recognizing Labor Day as an official national holiday. Labor Day marks the unofficial end of the summer season. Many colleges, secondary schools, and elementary schools begin classes immediately after Labor Day. State parks, campgrounds, and community swimming pools are all busy on Labor Day as vacationers take advantage of one last barbecued hamburger or hot dog. Many families travel to visit friends and relatives or enjoy a picnic to celebrate.

Menu

Carlos's Barbecue Burger

serves 6

This delicious recipe comes from Carlos, my brother from another mother.

Ingredients

- 2 lbs. ground beef
- 1 package dry onion mix
- Salt and pepper to taste
- 6 slices Swiss cheese
- 2 tomatoes, sliced
- 1 onion, sliced and grilled
- Lettuce pieces
- Your choice condiments
- 6 hamburger buns

> "Our attitude reflects on the work we do. When we seek creativity and satisfaction, we will find pleasure in all things, and it will become a labor of love."

Directions

Preheat grill. In a mixing bowl, combine ground beef, onion soup mix, salt, and pepper. Form mixture into 6 patties. Grill to your desired doneness. Turn once and add cheese. Serve with tomatoes, onion, lettuce, and your choice of condiments on buns.

Macaroni Salad

This recipe belonged to my mother-in-law, Edna. It's a great addition to summertime picnics and barbecues.

Ingredients

- 1 lb. macaroni
- 7 hardboiled eggs
- 1 (4-oz.) can chopped black olives
- 1 (4-oz.) can chopped pimentos
- 1 bunch green onions, chopped
- 2 cups mayonnaise
- Salt and pepper to taste
- Sprig of parsley for garnish
- Paprika

Directions

Cook macaroni till done, approximately 8 to 10 minutes, and drain. Chop 5 of the hardboiled eggs and slice 2 remaining eggs. In a large bowl, combine the macaroni, olives, pimentos, green onions, chopped hardboiled eggs, and mayonnaise, and season to taste with salt and pepper. Pour into serving bowl. Arrange egg slices on top. Add a sprig of parsley to the center and sprinkle with paprika for color.

Labor Day

Baked Beans

Ingredients

- 3 slices bacon
- ¼ cup onion, diced
- 1 Tbsp. ketchup
- 1 Tbsp. mustard
- 1 (15-oz.) can baked beans
- 2 Tbsp. brown sugar

Directions

Fry bacon until crisp. Set bacon to drain on paper towels until cool, and crumble. Add onion to drippings and cook until tender. Drain grease. Add ketchup, mustard, bacon pieces, beans and brown sugar to onion and simmer over low heat for 20 to 30 minutes.

7-Layer Salad

Serve this salad in a pretty, clear bowl, so your
friends and family can see all seven layers!

Ingredients

- 4 cups finely shredded lettuce
- 6 to 8 cherry tomatoes, halved
- 1 cup chopped celery
- ½ cup chopped onion
- 8 strips bacon, cooked and crumbled
- 1 (16-oz.) package frozen peas, thawed

Dressing

- ¾ cup mayonnaise
- ½ cup sour cream
- 1 Tbsp. lemon juice
- 1 cup grated cheddar cheese

Directions

Line bottom of serving bowl with chopped lettuce. Add tomato halves, with the outer
layer arranged so the cut side faces out. Next layer celery, onions, bacon, and peas. In
a separate bowl, mix together mayonnaise, sour cream, and lemon juice. Pour dressing
over top of salad, and top dressing with cheddar cheese. Cover with plastic wrap and
refrigerate overnight until ready to serve.

Labor Day

Dad's Homemade Ice Cream

My dad would make his special ice cream
for his grandkids. The grownups love it too!

Ingredients

- 6 eggs, beaten
- 3½ cups sugar
- 2 (12-oz.) cans
  evaporated milk
- 3 quarts milk
- 1½ tsp. vanilla

Directions

In a large bowl, stir together eggs and sugar and mix well. Add in milk and vanilla and continue to stir. Pour mixture into ice cream maker and process until frozen. If desired, place some of the frozen ice cream into plastic containers and store in the freezer for to enjoy at a later date. However, this ice cream is best served right away. Feel free to add your favorite fruit, berries, or other toppings.

Labor Day

Apple Pie

Ingredients

- 3 Tbsp. flour
- ½ cup sugar
- 1 tsp. cinnamon
- ⅛ tsp. salt
- 6 cups apple slices (I prefer a mix of Fuji and golden delicious)
- 2 uncooked pie crusts (see recipe on page 64)
- 2 Tbsp. butter

Directions

Preheat oven to 425 degrees.

Combine flour, sugar, cinnamon, and salt. In a large mixing bowl, combine apple slices and flour mixture, tossing to coat evenly. Spoon apples into an uncooked pie crust. Cut up small pieces of butter and place over top. Carefully place second pie crust over top of apples. Trim dough if necessary and flute edges to seal top crust and bottom crust together. Cut slits in the center of top crust to vent steam. Cover fluted edges with aluminum foil and bake for 40 minutes or until the pie crust is golden brown.

Flaky Pie Crust

This delicious crust handles well, rolls out easily,
and requires no chilling. Makes 2 (9-inch) pie crusts.

Ingredients

- 2 cups flour
- 1 tsp. salt
- ⅔ cup shortening
- 2 Tbsp. butter
- 5 Tbsp. ice water
- 1 Tbsp. vinegar

"If we but envision our dreams
we can accomplish them."

Directions

Mix flour and salt well. Cut in shortening and butter with pastry cutter until flour reaches a texture of small peas. Slowly add ice water and vinegar, mixing into flour with a fork, until dough holds together to form a ball. Divide in half. On a well-floured surface, roll out half of dough in a 12-inch circle and lift it carefully to a pie plate. This crust is very tender and may tear unless handled with care.

Paula Broberg

Labor Day

Halloween

"A Night of Costumes and Candy"

The word "Halloween" has its origins in the Catholic Church. It comes from a contracted corruption of "All Hallows Eve." November 1, **All Hallows Day,** also known as All Saints' Day, is a Catholic observance in honor of the church's saints. The custom of Halloween was brought to America in the 1840s by Irish immigrants trying to flee Ireland's potato famine. At that time, the favorite pranks in New England included tipping over outhouses and unhinging fence gates. The custom of **trick-or-treating** is thought to have originated with a ninth-century European custom called "souling." On November 2, known as "All Souls Day," early Christians would walk from village to village, begging for "soul cakes," which were made from square pieces of bread with currants. The more soul cakes the beggars received, the more prayers they could expect. Halloween allows children of all ages to be whatever they want, and on All Hallow's Eve, the crazier the costume, the better. **Costumes** transform far more than outward appearances—they allow people to forget themselves and to be whatever they can imagine and create. Many churches, Scouting programs, and other organizations have Halloween parties, haunted houses, and **pumpkin carving** events for the children.

Menu

"Hallo-Weenies"

This is a fun twist on the classic "pigs in a blanket." With a festive name and a little kick from the mustard, this special holiday treat is perfect for children of all ages.

Ingredients

- 1 package hot dogs
- 4 slices American cheese
- 4 Tbsp. mustard
- 1 can croissant rolls

Directions

Preheat oven 375 degrees.

Split hot dogs in half lengthwise, but make sure to not cut all the way through. Fill hot dogs with sliced cheese and mustard. Wrap one croissant roll around filled hot dog. Repeat process with remaining ingredients. Arrange croissant-wrapped hot dogs on a baking sheet and bake for approximately 20 minutes, or until golden brown.

Tomato Soup with Goop

This creamy concoction with melted blobs of cheese probably isn't helping the already iffy image of a bloodlike soup, but it goes over big at Halloween. Diners will enjoy playing with the blobs of goopy, melty cheese. But beware! This soup must be piping hot to melt the cheese, so use caution!

Ingredients

- 4 (10.75-oz.) cans uncondensed tomato soup
- 1 (12- to 14-oz.) block mozzarella cheese, cut into chunks
- 2 (5-oz.) packages mozzarella string cheese

Directions

Cook soup over medium-high heat, stirring occasionally, until mixture comes to boil, then lower heat. Set out warm bowls and add a chunk of mozzarella and one string cheese, torn into strips, to each bowl. Add a steaming ladleful of tomato soup into each bowl over cheese and serve.

Halloween

Grandma's Classic Favorites for Holidays and Seasons

Caramel Apples

serves 5

This is a delicious treat for Halloween or anytime in the fall, when apples are crisp and juicy. Golden delicious, Braeburn, McIntosh, and Granny Smith apples all work well for this recipe.

Ingredients

- 2 Tbsp. water
- 1 (14-oz.) package caramel candy
- 5 apples
- 5 wooden sticks

Directions

Line a cookie sheet with wax paper, and spray wax paper with cooking spray.

In a heavy pan over low heat, combine water and caramels, stirring occasionally with wooden spoon until smooth and melted. Meanwhile, wash and dry apples, remove stems, and pierce each apple with a wooden stick through the bottom. Dip apples into hot melted caramel. Shake off excess caramel, and gently roll apple around so caramel doesn't bunch up. Place caramel apple on prepared cookie sheet and let cool.

Tip: Don't overcook caramel, or it will get tough and hard to chew.

Bat Brew

Ingredients

- 1 (64-oz.) bottle grape juice
- ½ gallon lime sherbet
- 1 (2-liter) bottle lemon-lime soda

Directions

To serve, fill a glass half full with grape juice and add a scoop of lime sherbet. Fill the rest of the glass with lemon-lime soda. Stir slightly, mixing the bat brew.

Thanksgiving Day

"A Celebration of the Pilgrim's Tradition"

In 1621, the **pilgrims** observed the first Thanksgiving feast in Plymouth, Massachusetts. The meal lasted for three whole days! The **Native Americans** contributed wild game to the fare. The pilgrims shared food from their gardens. It was a time for giving thanks for their abundant harvest. For more than a century, the American people have celebrated this Thanksgiving holiday on the fourth Thursday each November with **traditions** of their own. **Family** and friends gather together on this holiday to share in celebration. Some families enjoy recipes that have been passed down from one generation to the next. Set a festive table with natural, beautiful fall colors of orange, golden yellow, and brown **autumn** leaves along with gourds, Indian corn, flowers, and spice-scented candles to create a warm atmosphere and appreciation for your **loved ones.** Give your guests the opportunity to count their blessings and give thanks to God for all they enjoy.

Menu

Papa Ken's Turkey and Stuffing

This family favorite is a recipe that my husband came up with. It's traditional, in our family, to serve Papa's turkey and dressing for our Thanksgiving dinner.

Ingredients

- 1 (6-oz.) box savory herb stuffing mix
- 1 (6-oz.) box cornbread stuffing mix
- 1 (6-oz.) box chicken stuffing mix
- 3 stalks celery, chopped into ½-inch pieces
- 1 large onion, chopped
- 3 lbs. fresh mushrooms, quartered
- 4 Tbsp. butter + extra for turkey
- 4 tsp. Worcestershire sauce
- 3 tsp. soy sauce
- 1 tsp. Tabasco sauce
- 2 tsp. sage
- 2 tsp. season salt
- 1 tsp. garlic salt
- 2 Tbsp. fresh parsley, chopped
- 1 tsp. pepper
- 1 (20-lb.) turkey, thawed, with neck and giblets removed

Directions

Preheat oven to 350 degrees.

In a large pot, add amount of water called for in stuffing package directions. Add celery, onion, mushrooms, butter, spice packets from stuffing, sauces, and remaining spices to water. Cover pot and bring liquid to a boil. Reduce heat and simmer for 5 to 10 minutes or until vegetables are tender. Add bread from mixes and stir well.

Rinse turkey well before stuffing. Place small pads of butter under turkey skin in a few places, sprinkle salt on top, and stuff with prepared dressing. Roast turkey for 5 to 6 hours, or until done. Let turkey stand for about 15 minutes before carving. Make sure to remove all the stuffing from neck area and cavity before turkey cools.

Place extra dressing in a ceramic baking dish, adding some of the drippings from cooked turkey for added flavor and moisture.

Christa's Yummy Mashed Potatoes

My granddaughter is a very creative cook. Try these potatoes served under a grilled chicken breast, and you will probably come back for seconds.

Ingredients

- 9 russet potatoes, peeled and quartered
- 4 Tbsp. butter
- ¾ cup hot milk
- 4 Tbsp. sour cream
- 2 oz. cream cheese, softened
- Salt and pepper

Directions

In a large pot of salted water, cook potatoes, covered, over medium heat until tender. Drain thoroughly. Add in butter and milk and beat with an electric mixer. Add sour cream and cream cheese and beat until fluffy. Add salt and pepper to taste. Serve while hot.

Creamed Peas and Cauliflower

Ingredients

- 1 head cauliflower
- 1 (10-oz.) box frozen peas
- 2 cups milk
- 3 Tbsp. flour
- 2 Tbsp. butter
- Salt and pepper to taste

"Let us observe this Thanksgiving Day in prayer with reverence and thankfulness. That we will rekindle in our hearts the will to preserve and acknowledge our blessings to our God that so generously gives them."

Directions

In a microwave-save bowl with vented cover, steam cauliflower in microwave for 3 to 4 minutes on high, or until cauliflower is tender and set aside. Cook peas in saucepan filled with a half-inch of water over medium heat until warmed through.

In a separate saucepan over medium heat, combine milk and flour and stir until slightly thickened. Add butter, salt, and pepper to taste. Add peas to sauce.

Place steamed cauliflower in the center of a large serving bowl and pour creamed peas around the sides of the cauliflower.

Glazed Yam Casserole

This is a holiday tradition in our family. This side dish is delicious with turkey and ham.

Ingredients

- 5 medium yams
- ¼ cup butter (½ cube)
- 2 eggs
- 1 tsp. vanilla
- ½ tsp. cinnamon
- ½ cup sugar
- 2 Tbsp. cream
- ¼ tsp. salt
- 3 Tbsp. flour
- ¼ cup butter (½ cube), softened
- ¾ cup brown sugar
- ½ cup pecans, chopped
- 1 cup corn flakes, crushed (optional)

Directions

Preheat oven to 375 degrees. Spray a 9x12-inch baking dish with non-stick cooking spray.

Scrub yams and cut in half lengthwise. Cover with water in a large saucepan with tight fitting lid and cook for 20 minutes or until tender. Drain, let cool, and remove skin. In a large bowl, beat yams, butter, eggs, vanilla, cinnamon, sugar, cream, and salt with an electric mixer until well blended. Spread yam mixture evenly in prepared dish. In a medium bowl, combine flour, soft butter, brown sugar, pecans, and crushed cornflakes together. Spread pecan mixture over top of yams. Cover with foil and bake until bubbly and hot all the way through, 20–25 minutes.

Thanksgiving

Grandma's Classic Favorites for Holidays and Seasons

Ten Layer Jell-O Salad

With all the beautiful colors of Jell-O, this salad is nice to serve in the fall of the year.

Ingredients

- 1 (3-oz.) package lemon Jell-O
- 1 (3-oz.) package lime Jell-O
- 1 (3-oz.) package orange Jell-O
- 1 (3-oz.) package strawberry Jell-O
- 1 (3-oz.) package raspberry Jell-O
- 5 cups boiling water
- 1 pint sour cream

"Thanksgiving Day is one of the holidays that is about its name. It is a day of giving thanks."

Directions

Start with the lightest color Jell-O and work to the darkest. For each box of Jell-O, dissolve 1 box gelatin with 1 cup boiling water. Melt sour cream in microwave for 30 seconds on high power. Mix ½ cup dissolved gelatin with ⅓ cup sour cream. Spread sour cream and Jell-O layer in a 9x13-inch dish and allow layer to set up. Mix the remaining dissolved Jell-O with ⅓ cup cold water and pour over set sour cream layer. Let second layer set up.

Repeat with remaining boxes of Jell-O. Keep salad refrigerated until ready to serve. Cut into squares so your guests can enjoy this delicious, multi-colored dessert!

Paula Broberg

Orange Cranberry Relish

Ingredients

- 1 package fresh cranberries
- 1 orange (with peel)
- 1 apple
- 1 cup sugar

Directions

In a blender, grind cranberries a few at a time and set aside in a bowl. Slice orange in half and remove white stem. Core apple and chop into small pieces. Mix orange, apple, and sugar in blender. Mix orange-apple mixture with ground cranberries and refrigerate until serving.

ten layer jell-o salad

Sherry's Best Rolls Ever

Sometimes my niece makes these easy yummy yeast rolls when she comes into town for a visit. I look forward to having them.

Ingredients

- 1 cup warm water
- ¼ cup sugar
- 2 packages dry yeast
- ½ cup salted butter (1 cube)
- 1 cup milk
- 5 to 6 cups flour

Directions

Preheat oven to 350 degrees.

In a medium bowl stir water and sugar together and add yeast. Let yeast mixture stand until it foams up above the top of the bowl, about 20 to 30 minutes.

Melt butter in a medium saucepan over medium heat, then add milk and bring to a boil. Remove from heat and let mixture cool until warm. In an extra large mixing bowl, gradually stir in flour with yeast until a creamy paste forms. Add the butter and milk. Stir in remaining flour, 1 cup at a time, until you are able to knead the dough without it sticking to your hands. Cover dough with a clean towel. Let rise to double in size.

Rolls can be made by simply pulling pieces of dough from the bowl and dropping them on a buttered cookie sheet. The size of the piece will depend on how large you want the rolls. Leave room for the dough to rise between each roll. Bake until the tops are brown and the rolls bounce back when you push on the center, 15 to 20 minutes.

Variations: Roll dough out to ¼ inch thickness, brush melted butter on the dough, and cut triangles to make crescents. This dough can also be used to make cinnamon rolls.

Paula Broberg

Thanksgiving

pecan pie, p. 80

Pecan Pie

Ingredients

- 1 cup pecans
- 1 pie crust
- 3 eggs, lightly beaten
- 1 cup brown sugar
- 1 tsp. vanilla
- 1 cup dark corn syrup
- 2 Tbsp. butter, melted

"On Thanksgiving, we feed more than our physical appetites. We feed our souls with a thankful heart."

Directions

Preheat oven to 325 degrees.

Spread the pecans evenly on the bottom of pie shell. In a mixing bowl, whisk eggs, brown sugar, vanilla, corn syrup, and melted butter together until well blended and let stand for 1 hour. Pour mixture over pecans and bake for 50 to 55 minutes or until filling sets.

Remove the pie from the oven and allow to cool for 10 minutes before slicing. Place a slice of the pie on the center of the plate, top with ice cream or whipped cream, and garnish with a mint leaf.

Christmas

"A Season of Faith, Hope, and Charity"

Christmastime is full of love, hope, and compassion for our fellowman. Everywhere you go, you can feel the spirit of Christmas, from holiday decorations, family gatherings, and Christmas carols to the wonderful smells of pine and cinnamon, delicious baked goodies, and the excitement of little children. There are so many ways to decorate your home for the holidays to make it warm and inviting, helping your family and guests feel special and loved. Christmas celebrations vary greatly among regions of the United States because of the variety of nationalities that have settled here. Different countries have given us their innovative ideas, which we have shared in. Austria gave us the favorite carol "Silent Night." Mexico brought the poinsettia plant. England contributed mistletoe and wassail. Germany gave the Christmas tree and Scandinavia the Yule log. We celebrate the birth of our Savior, Jesus Christ, more than two thousand years ago, as the most significant event in the history of the world.

Menu

Shrimp Cocktail

Ingredients

- 1 cup ketchup
- 2 tsp. Worcestershire sauce
- 1½ tsp. Tabasco sauce
- ½ tsp. garlic powder
- 2 Tbsp. horseradish
- 2 lbs. cooked shrimp
- ½ cup chopped celery

Directions

In medium bowl, combine all ingredients except shrimp and celery, mix well, and chill. Cut celery into small pieces.

To serve, arrange celery pieces in the bottom of a goblet. Top celery pieces with cocktail sauce in the center of goblet. Arrange cooled cooked shrimp around outside edge of goblet.

Prime Rib

serves 8

This high-quality cut of beef is often served at special occasions.
Scientific research proves that low temperature roasting
reduces shrinkage and therefore yields more portions.

Ingredients

- 1 (10-lb.) prime rib
- Kosher salt
- 1½ Tbsp. chopped garlic
- Fresh ground pepper
- ½ cup water

Directions

Preheat oven to 350 degrees.

Rub beef with salt and sprinkle all sides with chopped garlic and pepper.
Pour water in bottom of roasting pan, and set seasoned beef in pan with
ribs down. Cover with aluminum foil. Bake for about 45 minutes. Reduce
oven temperature to 325 degrees and finish baking for approximately 45
more minutes. This will cook your prime rib to rare in middle and medium
on the ends. When meat is done let stand for about 15 minutes before
carving. Cook longer if you like your prime rib more done.

Christmas

Paula Broberg

Garlic Mashed Potatoes

Ingredients

- 9 medium potatoes, peeled and quartered
- 1 tsp. crushed garlic
- 3 oz. cream cheese, softened
- 3 Tbsp. butter
- ¼ cup milk at room temperature
- Salt and pepper to taste

Directions

In medium saucepan, boil potatoes in salted water until tender. Drain and return to saucepan. Add garlic, cream cheese, and butter, and beat with electric mixer. Add milk until potatoes reach desired consistency. Add salt and pepper to taste.

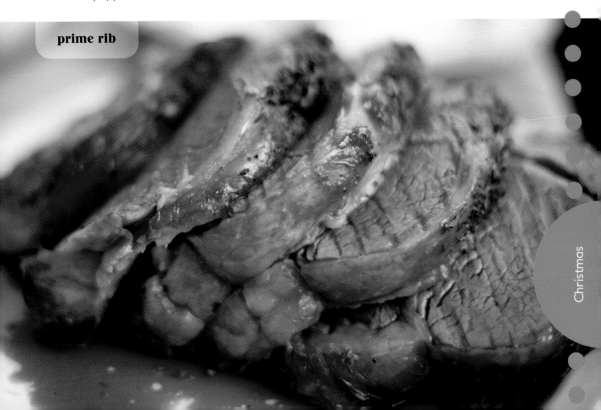

prime rib

Potato Rolls

These rolls are "holiday homemade style," according to my dear friend Carolyn Ducret. At least that's what she said when she walked through my door the year we spent Christmas in Hawaii. These rolls make the whole house smell so good, and are they ever so yummy!

Ingredients

- ⅓ cup shortening
- 1 cup sugar
- 1 potato, boiled and mashed
- 1½ cups milk, scalded
- 1 yeast cake, dissolved in 1 cup lukewarm water
- 2 eggs, beaten
- 1½ Tbsp. salt
- 2 cups sifted flour + 5 to 6 cups flour

Directions

Mix together shortening, sugar, mashed potato, and scalded milk and cool to tepid. Add dissolved yeast cake, eggs, salt, and 2 cups sifted flour and beat thoroughly. Gradually work in enough flour to make a soft dough. Grease dough, cover, and chill in refrigerator overnight. (Dough will keep in refrigerator for up to 3 weeks.)

When ready to bake, remove desired amount of dough and roll into balls. Let rise 1 to 2 hours. Bake at 425 degrees for 20 minutes. Serve warm.

Mushrooms and Pearl Onions

Ingredients

- 2 Tbsp. + ¼ tsp. butter
- 1 lb. small fresh mushrooms
- 1 (10-oz.) can pearl onions
- 2 cups milk
- 3 Tbsp. flour
- 6 to 8 oz. Velveeta cheese
- Salt and pepper to taste

> "The key to happiness belongs to each of us on earth. He who seeks after faith, hope, and charity can touch countless hearts with this gift we each can possess."

Directions

Melt 2 Tbsp. butter in a medium saucepan and add in whole mushrooms. When mushrooms are part way cooked through, add onions. When onions and mushrooms are warmed through, set aside.

In a separate saucepan over medium heat, stir milk and flour until slightly thickened. Add remaining butter, cheese, salt, and pepper. Pour cheese sauce over mushrooms and onions and serve warm.

Christmas

Homemade Holiday Eggnog Pie

This is a holiday dessert shared by my dear friend Barbara Welsh, who said that this recipe is so easy, she wasn't sure if I'd want to put it in a cookbook. But it tastes too good not to include it, so this is for all you eggnog lovers out there.

Ingredients

- 1 unbaked pie crust (see recipe on page 64)
- 1 (3.4-oz.) box instant vanilla pudding
- 2 cups eggnog
- ½ pint heavy whipping cream, whipped
- Nutmeg

Directions

Preheat oven to 325 degrees.

Bake pie crust for 10 to 12 minutes or until lightly golden brown. Set aside until cool. In a chilled mixing bowl, mix pudding and eggnog until thickened. Pour pudding mixture into cooled pie crust, top with whipped cream, and sprinkle with nutmeg. Refrigerate for at least 3 hours before serving.

Christmas

Paula Broberg

Mimi's Cheesecake

Through the years, this has been a favorite of my children and grandchildren for Christmas or any other time of the year. They loved it so much that they begged me to make enough so each one of them could have their own cake! This is a perfect cheesecake—I have not tried any other I liked better.

Ingredients

- 20 graham crackers, crushed into fine powder
- ½ cup (1 cube) butter, melted
- 1 lb. cream cheese, softened
- ½ cup + 1 Tbsp. sugar
- ½ tsp. vanilla

- 1 (8-oz. can) crushed pineapple, reserving 1 Tbsp. + 1 tsp. juice
- 2 eggs, separated
- ⅛ tsp. ground cinnamon
- 1 cup sour cream

directions on page 90

Directions for Mimi's Cheesecake

Preheat oven to 300 degrees.

Mix graham cracker crumbs and melted butter and press into a buttered 9-inch pie plate, building crust up sides of the plate. Reserve 2 Tbsp. of mix and set aside.

In a medium bowl, beat together cream cheese, ½ cup sugar, vanilla, and 1 tablespoon. pineapple juice until smooth. Beat in egg yolks and add cinnamon. In a separate bowl, beat egg whites until stiff, but not dry. Fold egg whites into filling. Pour filling into crust and bake for 45 minutes.

While cheesecake is baking, make topping: beat 1 tablespoon sugar, 1 teaspoon. pineapple juice, and sour cream until smooth.

Remove cheesecake from oven. Spread drained pineapple over top of hot cheesecake. Spread topping over pineapple and sprinkle reserved graham cracker crumbs over topping. Return cheesecake to oven and bake 10 minutes longer. Let cheesecake cool completely. Chill in refrigerator for at least 3 hours before serving.

This recipe can be made without pineapple with just a couple of ingredient changes. Substitute 1 teaspoon lemon rind for crushed pineapple, 1 tablespoon lemon juice for pineapple juice in filling, and 1 teaspoon vanilla for pineapple juice in topping.

New Year's Eve

"A Reflection of a Year Gone By"

At the end of a year and the start of the year to come, New Year's Eve is a time to celebrate the resolutions and goals of things in our lives we want to change or accomplish in the coming year—a **new year** and a new beginning for each of us. Each day, we create the person, the self, we will become. And each day, we can choose to change that future person into what ever we choose to become. Each day is a new beginning—another chance to learn more about others, to laugh more than we did before, to **accomplish** more than we thought we could, and to be more than we were before. On New Year's Eve, it is traditional to greet the New Year at **midnight** and celebrate it in the company of friends and family. Many hold parties with dancing, singing songs like "Auld Lang Syne," and ringing in the New Year with a toast, and a kiss shared with that special someone. Whether you share the evening with large crowd or stay at home with your sweetheart, here is the perfect menu for you.

Menu

Caesar Salad

Ingredients

- 1 large clove garlic
- 6 anchovies, rinsed
- 1½ Tbsp. Dijon mustard
- 1 tsp. Worcestershire sauce
- ¼ cup fresh lemon juice
- ¼ cup olive oil
- 1 egg
- ½ cup Parmesan cheese + 3 Tbsp. for garnish
- 1 head romaine lettuce
- ½ tsp. fresh ground pepper
- Seasoned croutons

Directions

In a food processor, mince garlic and anchovies. Add mustard, Worcestershire sauce, lemon juice, oil, egg, and ½ cup grated Parmesan cheese. Process till thick and smooth. Rinse lettuce and pat dry with paper towels. Tear into bite-size pieces and place in salad bowl. Pour dressing over lettuce and sprinkle ground black pepper, croutons, and remaining Parmesan cheese over top of salad. Toss lightly and serve.

London Broil

Ingredients

- ¾ cup olive oil
- ¼ cup red wine vinegar
- ¼ cup red wine
- 5 garlic cloves, chopped
- 1 (3-lb.) flank steak

Directions

In a 9x12-inch pan, mix together all ingredients but steak. Poke steak with a with a fork on both sides, place in pan with marinade and marinate in refrigerator for 2 to 3 hours, turning steak over every hour.

Since a flank steak can get tough if overcooked, it is best grilled or pan-fried to medium-rare. Cook to your liking. Use meat thermometer to check for doneness. To serve, slice steak against the grain.

New Year's Eve

King Crab Legs

This is the Big Daddy of crabs. It doesn't get any better than this.

Ingredients

- 2 to 3 lbs. king crab legs, fresh or thawed
- ¼ cup (½ cube) butter, melted
- 1 lemon

Directions

Rinse and dry crab legs. In a large pot filled with an inch or two of water, steam legs for approximately 15 minutes. Use kitchen shears to cut down the sides of the soft shell to expose the meat, allowing meat to be removed easily.

To serve, place meat on a warm plate. Serve with small bowls of hot melted butter and a squeeze of lemon for dipping. It's so good!

Rice Pilaf

Ingredients

- 5 sticks vermicelli or thin spaghetti
- 1 Tbsp. light olive oil
- 1 (14-oz.) can mushrooms, drained
- 1 cup long grain rice
- 1 (14.5-oz.) can chicken broth
- ½ tsp. onion flakes
- ½ tsp. salt
- ½ tsp. pepper

Directions

Preheat oven to 350 degrees.

Break pasta into small pieces, and place them in large skillet with olive oil over medium-low heat. Watching carefully to prevent burning, stir constantly until light golden brown. Pour pasta into an 8x8-inch baking dish. Add remaining ingredients, stir, and bake, covered, for 60 minutes.

Chocolate Cream Cheese Mousse

serves 12

Ingredients

- 1½ lbs. semisweet baking chocolate
- 4 oz. cream cheese
- 3 egg yolks
- 4 cups milk
- 1½ oz. corn starch
- 1 cup sugar
- 1½ pints heavy cream, whipped

Directions

Melt chocolate and cream cheese in a double boiler or a saucepan sitting in a shallow pan of water. In a small bowl, beat egg yolks with 2 tablespoons milk and cornstarch. In a separate saucepan, mix sugar with remaining milk, and bring to boil over low heat, stirring often to prevent scorching. Add cornstarch mixture to boiling milk and continue to cook over low heat, stirring constantly, until mixture reaches the consistency of custard. Add melted chocolate and cream cheese. Remove from heat and let cool. When thoroughly cool, fold whipped cream into mousse. Spoon into cups or parfait glasses and chill.

mushroom soup, p. 102

Spring Season

"Celebrating the Rebirth of Nature"

Springtime is my favorite time of the year. It is a time to open up the house and let that fresh air in, to start cleaning projects I've been waiting all winter to do: cleaning windows, touching up paint, and others. Spring is the time to go outside and get your **garden** and flower beds cleaned up so you can see all the bulbs you planted last fall starting to pop up through the earth. The trees are starting to show off their **colors** with their pink and white blossoms. Flowering shrubs start to open their buds. Springtime is heard as much as it is seen. The birds and other creatures are all busy making new homes and getting ready to start families. Spring is sweet to the senses and easy to celebrate. It's a great time to lighten the load, peel off the heavy winter clothing, and shed a few of those pounds we might have put on. Start going on walks and enjoy being **outdoors** after a quiet winter. Spring is also the perfect time to make some of those recipes that are light and luscious for lunch or dinner.

Menu

Papa's French Toast

Ingredients

- 2 eggs
- 4 Tbsp. milk
- ¼ cup powdered sugar
- ½ cube (1 cube) butter
- 1 loaf French bread, sliced
- Syrup

Directions

In a small bowl, mix eggs and milk together. Add 1 tablespoon powdered sugar and mix well. In a skillet, heat 1 tablespoon butter. Dip bread slices, one at a time, into egg mixture, taking care not to over soak, and place into skillet on medium heat. Brown bread on one side and sprinkle with powdered sugar. Turn bread and brown on other side. Repeat with remaining bread slices and egg mixture. Serve French toast with remaining butter and syrup.

Spring

Mimi's Mushroom Soup

Fresh mushrooms transform even the simplest dish into something special. That's the magic of mushrooms.

Ingredients

- ½ cup (1 cube) butter
- 1 onion, chopped
- 1 stalk celery and tops, finely chopped
- ½ cup baby carrots, thinly sliced
- 1 lb. mushrooms, thinly sliced
- 1 clove garlic, chopped
- ½ cup flour
- 2 cups chicken broth
- ½ cup white wine
- ¼ cup sherry
- 1 bay leaf
- 2 tsp. fresh thyme
- 1 cup half and half or ½ cup milk
- Sea salt and white pepper to taste
- Fresh parsley, chopped
- ½ cup cream

Directions

Melt butter in a large stockpot and add onion, celery, carrots, mushrooms, and garlic, and sauté until slightly tender. Add flour, making a roux, and cook for 5 minutes.

Add chicken broth, wine, and sherry, whipping mixture vigorously with a wire whisk until slightly thickened. Add bay leaf and thyme, and simmer until vegetables are tender. Add half and half or milk and salt and pepper to taste. Pour into hot bowls and top with a little parsley and a dash of cream.

Paula Broberg

Randi's Cheesy Broccoli and Cauliflower

This is a simple and scrumptious way to eat your vegetables. My granddaughter has prepared this side dish, combining the two different veggies together to put a different twist on her recipe.

Ingredients

- 1 lb. fresh broccoli, cut into florets
- 1 head cauliflower, cut into pieces
- 3 Tbsp. butter
- 1 cup fresh Parmesan cheese, grated
- Salt and pepper to taste

Directions

In a medium saucepan, steam or boil broccoli and cauliflower in water until tender. Drain off water and add butter, Parmesan, salt, and pepper. Stir until cheese is melted. With an electric mixer, mix vegetables until texture resembles mashed potatoes, and serve. These are delicious!

Spring

Chicken Broccoli Casserole

Ingredients

- 2 large chicken breasts
- 1 large crown broccoli
- 1 cup sour cream
- 1 cup mayonnaise
- 2 (10.75-oz.) cans cream of chicken soup
- 1 tsp. lemon juice
- 1 cup shredded cheddar cheese
- ½ cup bread crumbs
- Parmesan cheese, freshly grated

Directions

Preheat oven to 350 degrees.

In a stockpot, add enough water to cover chicken breasts, and cook over medium heat until tender. Remove chicken and set aside. Cut broccoli into florets and add to stockpot with chicken stock. Cook until broccoli is tender and drain. Dice cooked chicken breasts. In a 9x12-inch baking dish, arrange chicken pieces on the bottom and layer broccoli over chicken. In a medium bowl, mix together sour cream, mayonnaise, cream of chicken soup, and lemon juice and pour mixture over top of broccoli. Top with cheddar cheese, bread crumbs, and Parmesan cheese. Bake until bubbly, about 30 minutes. Serve hot.

tarragon chicken

Tarragon Chicken in Mushroom Sauce

This is one of the most delicious chicken dishes I have ever made. Everyone raves about it and wants the recipe.

Ingredients

- 5 Tbsp. olive oil
- 5 Tbsp. butter
- 1 whole chicken, cut up
- 2 Tbsp. tarragon
- 1 Tbsp. beau monde seasoning
- 1 lb. mushrooms, sliced
- ½ cup flour, for dusting

- ½ cup white wine (optional)
- 3 cloves garlic, chopped
- 1 cup chicken broth
- 2 cups sour cream
- 1 (14-oz.) box minute rice
- 1 cup green onions, with greens, chopped

Directions

Preheat oven to 350 degrees.

In a cast iron skillet, heat 3 Tbsp. oil and 2 Tbsp. butter over medium heat. Dredge chicken pieces in flour and sprinkle with tarragon and beau monde. Brown chicken pieces on each side and set aside. In same skillet, add remaining ingredients except chicken broth, sour cream, rice, and green onions. Simmer just until mushrooms are halfway cooked. Place browned chicken pieces in a large Dutch oven, pour sauce over top, add chicken broth, and bake for 45 minutes. Arrange roasted chicken pieces on platter. Add sour cream to cast iron skillet and stir well over low heat until blended. Make minute rice as directed on box. Pour sauce over chicken and rice and sprinkle green onions on top. Serve while hot.

Spring

Carol's Monkey Bread

Everyone should be blessed with a good friend
like Carol Moschetti. She is a very special lady.

Ingredients

- 4 tsp. cinnamon
- ⅓ cup sugar
- 8 oz. cream cheese, softened
- 2 (12-oz.) cans Buttermilk biscuits
- ½ cup (1 cube) butter
- 1 cup brown sugar
- ⅔ cup pecans or walnuts

Directions

Preheat oven to 350 degrees.

Mix cinnamon, sugar, and cream cheese together in a small bowl. Pull apart
biscuits and arrange on a bread board. Using a spoon, press down each
biscuit to make an indentation. Fill each indentation with the cream cheese
mixture. In a saucepan melt butter and brown sugar together until smooth,
stirring constantly. Sprinkle nuts in the bottom of a bundt pan and arrange
biscuits in pan. Biscuits will overlap. Pour brown sugar mixture over biscuits
and bake for 30 minutes or until golden brown. Cool 5 minutes before serving.

To serve, invert bundt pan on serving plate and pull biscuits apart into
individual servings.

Spring

Frozen Strawberry Fruit Salad

This is a wonderful dish that can be served as a side
salad with a meal or as a after dinner dessert.

Ingredients

- 8 oz. cream cheese, softened
- ¾ cup sugar
- 2 cups strawberries, sliced and smashed
- 1 (15-oz.) can crushed pineapple, drained
- 6 bananas, smashed
- 1 (9-oz.) carton whipped topping

Directions

In a large bowl, combine cream cheese and sugar until smooth. Add remaining
ingredients and mix well. Pour into a 9x13-inch pan, cover, and freeze overnight
or until ready to serve.

Spring

Lemon Curd

Ingredients

- Juice and zest of 2 large lemons
- 1½ cups sugar
- 3 large eggs, lightly beaten
- ½ cup (1 cube) butter

Directions

In a heavy saucepan or double boiler over medium-low heat, combine lemon zest and juice, sugar, and eggs. Stir constantly until thickened, approximately 5 minutes. Do not allow mixture to boil or burn in the bottom of pan. Add butter and stir until well blended. Store, chilled, in a container with a tight-fitting lid until ready to use. Makes 1½ cups. Will keep approximately 2 weeks in the refrigerator.

"Cooking is and always will be a creative opportunity, because you are making something out of nothing."

Lemon Jell-O Cake

This is for all you lemon lovers. This cake can be served two ways: glazed or frosted. I like to serve it glazed in a 9x13-inch glass baking dish or as frosted cupcakes. Either way it's lemonlicious.

Ingredients

- 1 box lemon cake mix
- ¾ cup oil
- 4 eggs
- 1 tsp. lemon extract
- 1 (3-oz.) package lemon Jell-O
- 1 cup boiling water

Glaze

- 2 cups powdered sugar
- Juice of 2 large lemons

Frosting

- 2 cups powdered sugar sifted
- 4 oz. cream cheese
- 4 Tbsp. lemon curd (see page 108)
- 2 tsp. lemon rind
- Juice of 1 small lemon, strained

Directions

Preheat oven to 350 degrees.

In a large bowl, combine cake mix, oil, eggs, and lemon extract with an electric mixer until well blended. In a separate bowl, stir Jell-O powder and boiling water until dissolved. Add Jell-O to cake mixture and continue to beat 2 or 3 more minutes. Pour cake batter into a 9x13-inch baking pan or lined cupcake pan. Bake cake for 30 to 35 minutes, or cupcakes for 20 minutes.

While waiting for cake(s), make glaze and frosting (if desired). For glaze: mix sugar and lemon juice until powder sugar dissolves completely. For frosting: with an electric mixer, mix all ingredients until smooth.

Remove cake(s) from oven. While hot, prick with fork to make holes all around top of cake to allow glaze to seep down. Pour glaze over top of cake. When making frosted cupcakes, you will not need as much glaze. Allow cake(s) to cool before frosting.

Spring

Paula Broberg

Cinnamon Apples

Ingredients

- 8 Granny Smith apples
- 4 Tbsp. brown sugar
- 2 tsp. butter, melted
- 1 tsp. lemon juice
- 2 tsp. Red Hots cinnamon candy

Directions

Preheat oven to 350 degrees.

Wash apples and slice in half, hollowing out cores. Arrange in shallow baking dish, cut side up. In a small bowl, mix together brown sugar, butter, and lemon juice and pour over apples. Sprinkle cinnamon candies over apples and bake for 25 minutes or until apples are tender. Serve warm.

Spring

Grandma's Classic Favorites for Holidays and Seasons

Strawberry Pie

This sweet and scrumptious dessert was served to me by a wonderful cook (and special lady) named Barb Welsh in Gold Beach, Oregon. This has become one of my favorite pies. Thanks, Barb!

Ingredients

- 1 cup water
- 1 cup sugar
- 3 Tbsp. + 1 tsp. cornstarch
- 3 Tbsp. strawberry Jell-O powder
- 1 quart strawberries, washed, stemmed, and halved
- 1 baked pie crust (see page 64)
- 1 pint heavy whipping cream, whipped

Directions

In a large saucepan over medium heat, combine water, sugar, and cornstarch, stirring constantly until thickened. Add Jell-O powder to syrup and cook for a few minutes. Allow to cool. Add strawberry halves and mix well. Pour strawberry filling into baked pie crust. Top with whipped cream and refrigerate. Serve cold.

Spring

Summer Season

"Having Fun in the Sun"

Plant a garden so your family can enjoy the fruits of your labor throughout the season. Tuck in a variety of herbs and edible flowers around your vegetables to add beauty and creativity to your summer meals. Try using edible flowers to decorate cakes, float in a punch bowl with fruit punch, decorate **ice cream,** or garnish dessert plates. You can even decorate your napkins with strings of these beautiful edible flowers or just scatter the petals around the table with an arrangement in the center. Pansies, day lilies, violets, rose petals, jump-ups, forget-me-nots, honeysuckle, nasturtiums, and herb flowers are all edible. To celebrate summer, with all the enthusiasm that it brings, make up some refreshing, festive, and fun foods your family and friends can all enjoy for that perfect picnic, **barbeque,** or backyard party. Enjoy a "Lavender-and-Lace" party on a summer afternoon. Ask guests to wear lavender, and decorate your table appropriately. You can even scent whipping cream by pouring the cream over lavender **blossoms,** letting it sit overnight, and then whipping. Use on a fruit salad or serve with scones.

Menu

Corn Chowder

Ingredients

- 4 slices bacon
- 2 slices salt pork
- 1 medium onion, minced
- ½ cup chopped leeks
- 2 tsp. flat leaf parsley
- ¼ cup unbleached flour
- 3 cups chicken broth

- 4 cups fresh sweet corn kernels, half mashed and half whole
- 2 cups Yukon potatoes, diced
- 2 cups half and half
- 2 Tbsp. butter
- Coarse sea salt and white pepper to taste
- ½ cup grated mild cheddar cheese (optional)

Directions

In a 12-cup cast iron pot or heavy bottomed soup pot, fry bacon and salt pork until crisp. Drain bacon and salt pork on a paper towel and set aside. In same pot, use bacon renderings to sauté onion and leeks until lightly browned. Stir in fresh parsley. Sprinkle flour over onion mixture and cook for a few minutes to make a lightly browned roux. Slowly add broth to roux and continue stirring to incorporate the broth into roux, breaking up any flour clumps to make a smooth sauce.

Bring liquid to a boil. Reduce heat and simmer for 20 minutes. Return heat to medium-high and add corn and potatoes. Bring liquid back to a boil. Reduce heat to a simmer. Cook chowder at a low simmer for 30 more minutes or until potatoes are fork-tender. Add half-and-half and butter, stirring constantly over low heat until chowder is steaming hot. Remove from heat and add salt and pepper to taste.

To serve, sprinkle individual servings with reserved bacon and some extra sprigs of fresh, flat-leaf parsley. For a cheesy corn chowder, add ½ cup grated cheddar cheese when you add the half and half and butter.

Summer

Paula Broberg

Summer Pea Salad

Ingredients

- 4 slices bacon
- 1 (10-oz.) package frozen peas, thawed and drained
- 1 cup shredded cheddar cheese
- 3 hard-cooked eggs, peeled and chopped
- 5 Tbsp. mayonnaise
- 3 tsp. freshly squeezed lemon juice
- Salt and fresh ground pepper to taste

"Families are the flowers in the gardens of our life."

Directions

In a large skillet, cook bacon over medium heat until crisp. Transfer to a paper towel-lined plate to drain. Let cool. In a medium serving bowl, combine crumbled bacon, peas, cheese, and eggs. Stir in mayonnaise and lemon juice. Add salt and pepper to taste. Serve immediately or refrigerate until ready to serve.

corn chowder

Summer

Robin's Spaghetti

My daughter-in-law got this recipe from her grandmother.
When we go to visit, she always makes this for us.

Ingredients

- 1½ lbs. ground beef
- 1 medium onion, chopped
- 2 cloves garlic, minced
- 9 large mushrooms, sliced OR
  1 (15-oz.) can sliced mushrooms
- 2 (15-oz.) cans tomato sauce
- 2 (15-oz.) can stewed tomatoes
- 2 (15-oz.) cans water
- ½ Tbsp. oregano
- 2 bay leaves
- Sea salt and fresh ground pepper
- 1½ lbs. vermicelli
- 1 cup fresh grated Parmesan cheese

Directions

In a large cast iron skillet over medium heat, cook ground beef, onion, and garlic until meat has browned. Transfer beef mixture to a large pot and add mushrooms, tomato sauce, stewed tomatoes, water, oregano, bay leaves, and salt and pepper to taste. Stir to combine and bring to a low simmer. When ready to serve, bring a pot of salted water to a boil. Add vermicelli to boiling water and cook 5 to 7 minutes or until *al dente* and drain. Add pasta to sauce and mix well. Serve on a platter topped with fresh grated Parmesan cheese.

Cranberry Chicken Salad

serves 4

This scrumptious entrée is perfect for a summer night. It's cool and easy.

Ingredients

- 4 cups cooked chicken, cooled and cut into chunks
- 1 (8-oz.) can pineapple chunks
- 2 stalks celery, thinly sliced
- 1 green onion, thinly sliced
- ½ cup toasted slivered almonds
- ½ cup cranberries
- 1 cup green grapes, whole
- ½ cup mayonnaise
- ½ cup ranch dressing

Directions

In a large bowl, combine all ingredients except mayonnaise and ranch dressing. In a separate bowl mix mayonnaise and ranch dressing and pour over chicken mixture. Mix well. Refrigerate, covered, until ready to serve. Serve on a lettuce leaf.

Summer

Stuffed Zucchini

This is a delicious way to use those overgrown zucchinis from your garden.

Ingredients

- 1 large (12-inch or longer) zucchini
- 2 Tbsp. butter
- 1 clove garlic chopped
- 1 lb. ground beef
- 2 eggs
- ½ onion, chopped
- ¼ green bell pepper, chopped
- 1 slice bread, torn into pieces
- ½ cup instant oats
- ⅛ cup milk
- 3 Tbsp. ketchup
- 1 Tbsp. Dijon mustard
- ¼ tsp. Worcestershire sauce
- ½ can stewed tomatoes, drained
- 1 tsp. salt
- ¾ tsp. pepper
- 1 slice Monterey jack cheese

Directions

Preheat oven to 350 degrees.

Cut zucchini in half, lengthwise, and spoon out seeds. In a skillet over medium heat, mix butter, garlic, and scooped-out zucchini, and cook for approximately 5 minutes. Drain off juice and transfer mixture to a large mixing bowl. Add remaining ingredients except cheese. Mix well and stuff into zucchini shells. Arrange stuffed zucchini in a baking dish, and baked, covered, for 35 minutes. Remove from oven and top with cheese. Bake, uncovered, for another 10 minutes or until cheese melts. Serve while hot!

Paula Broberg

Mimi's Lemon Shrimp Pasta

Ingredients

- 1 lb. fettuccine noodles
- 2 Tbsp. olive oil
- 2 Tbsp. butter
- 8 cloves garlic, crushed
- 1 cup baby 'bella mushrooms, sliced
- 1 tsp. thyme
- 1 tsp. basil
- 1 tsp. oregano

- 2 lbs. medium shrimp, cleaned and deveined
- 1 lemon, juiced
- 10 grape tomatoes, sliced
- ¾ cups cream
- 1 Tbsp. fresh parsley, chopped
- Fresh grated Parmesan cheese
- Zest of 1 lemon

Directions

Prepare pasta according to package directions. In a large, nonstick skillet over medium heat, add olive oil, butter, garlic, mushrooms, thyme, basil, and oregano and stir well for 10 minutes, making sure not to burn garlic. Add shrimp, lemon juice, and tomatoes, and simmer for 5 to 10 minutes, or until shrimp are pink. Mix cream and pasta into shrimp mixture. Before serving, sprinkle pasta with parsley, cheese, and lemon zest. Serve while hot.

Zucchini Bread

Ingredients

- 2 cups sugar
- ½ cup oil
- ½ cup applesauce
- 3 eggs
- 1 Tbsp. salt
- 2½ tsp. cinnamon
- 2 cups flour
- 1 tsp. baking soda
- 1 tsp. baking powder
- 2 tsp. vanilla
- 1½ cups walnuts, chopped
- 2½ cups zucchini, grated

Directions

Preheat oven to 325 degrees.

In a large bowl using an electric mixer, cream sugar and oil until smooth. Add applesauce and eggs to mixture and mix well. In a separate bowl, mix dry ingredients together, and add gradually to wet ingredients until well combined. Add vanilla and fold in nuts.

Squeeze as much water out of grated zucchini as possible, and mix zucchini into batter. Pour batter into greased floured bread pan and bake for 35 minutes or until a toothpick inserted in the center of bread comes out clean. Can be baked in small bread loafs.

Summer

Vichyssoise Soup

Ingredients

- 3 large leeks, chopped
- 1 small onion, chopped
- 1½ lbs. potatoes, peeled and quartered
- 4 cups chicken broth
- 2 cups half and half
- ¼ cup (½ cube) butter
- 1 tsp. fresh parsley, chopped
- Salt and pepper to taste
- Chopped chives, for garnish

Directions

In a medium saucepan, sauté leeks and onion in butter until tender. Add potatoes and chicken broth, bring to a boil, then reduce heat and simmer uncovered for 40 to 45 minutes until potatoes are tender. Place potato mixture into blender and process until pureed. Add half-and-half, butter, and parsley and mix well. Add salt and pepper to taste. Pour into a container with a tight-fitting lid and chill for at least 3 hours or overnight. Serve in clear, long-stemmed goblets and garnish with a few chives on top.

Summer

Grandma's Classic Favorites for Holidays and Seasons

Fresh Fruit Tart

Ingredients

Crust

- 2 cups vanilla wafers, crushed
- ½ cup (1 cube) butter, melted

Filling

- 8 oz. cream cheese
- ¼ cup sugar
- 2 tsp. lemon juice
- ½ cup whipping cream
- Assorted fruit (strawberries, blueberries, blackberries, raspberries, red or green grapes)
- ¼ cup strawberry preserves
- 1 Tbsp. water
- Mint leaves (optional)

Directions

Preheat oven to 350 degrees.

In a small bowl, combine crushed wafers and butter, then press mixture into bottom and sides of 10-inch removable tart pan. Bake for 8 minutes or until light brown and let cool.

Combine cream cheese, sugar, and lemon juice with an electric mixer. Add in whipping cream and beat on high until light and fluffy. Spread in shell and chill for at least 3 hours. Arrange fruit on top of chilled filling. Combine strawberry preserves with water and brush over top. Garnish with mint leaves and serve.

Frozen Lemon Cream Pie

Ingredients

Crust

- 10 graham crackers, finely crushed
- ½ box vanilla wafers, finely crushed
- ½ cup (1 cube) butter, melted

Filling

- 1 (14-oz.) can sweetened condensed milk
- 8 oz. cream cheese, softened
- ⅓ cup lemon juice
- ¼ tsp. lemon extract
- Zest of 2 lemons

Directions

Spray pie plate with nonstick cooking spray. Combine crushed crackers, crushed wafers, and melted butter. Press crumbs into pie plate. In a medium bowl, mix together remaining ingredients until well blended and pour mix into piecrust. Sprinkle a little lemon zest on top. Freeze until ready to serve.

fresh fruit tart

Summer

Blackberry Cobbler

Traditionally, when the blackberries were in season and it was time for picking, my mother, my two daughters, my five granddaughters, and I would all go berry picking in Oregon, where I live. We would get our old clothes on and wear long-sleeve shirts to protect our arms. Well, in August, it gets pretty hot, so we would get up and go out early in the mornings to pick.

This recipe was my Aunt Evelyn's. It's easy and so good served hot from the oven with a little half-and-half or whipping cream poured over the top, and you can't go wrong with a scoop of vanilla ice cream. Any way you like it, it's a hit.

Ingredients

- 4 cups blackberries, washed
- ½ cup sugar to taste

Crust

- ¾ cup (1½ cubes) melted butter
- 1½ cups self-rising flour
- 1½ cups sugar
- 1½ cups whole milk

"You can either complain that the blackberries have thorns or thank God that the thorns have blackberries."

Directions

Preheat oven to 350 degrees.

In a large saucepan over medium heat, cook blackberries and sugar for 5 to 10 minutes, stirring until sugar is dissolved. In a 9x13-inch glass baking dish, melt butter in microwave. In a large bowl, mix flour, sugar, and milk together and stir until well blended. Pour into buttered baking dish. Top batter with sweetened blackberries. Bake cobbler for 45 to 50 minutes.

Paula Broberg

Fall Season

"Enjoying Autumn's Bounty"

Fall is an excellent opportunity for enjoying the last of the **harvest** from your garden, whether you freeze or can to enjoy your fresh produce for the rest of the year. Did you know you can make your own herbal vinegar? Use herbs or herb flowers picked at the peak of their flavors. Red or white vinegar is preferable. Use a glass jar to let light penetrate the vinegar while brewing and retaining flavor. Use a ceramic or stainless steal saucepan, because other metal pans react with vinegar. Use cork to seal your jars or bottles. Mince your choice of herbs and heat vinegar to near-boiling. Bruise herbs as you add them to the jar. Allow vinegar to steep for two weeks, then strain and rebottle. Add fresh sprigs of whole herbs to the bottle for decoration. Fall is also a wonderful time to learn the art of canning. Sure, it may be time consuming and sometimes tedious, but canning does more than store food. . . . It **nourishes** the soul. Try cooking up something special to **cozy** up with on those cool autumn nights. May the garden of your life always be filled with three important seeds: faith, hope, and charity.

Menu

Mary's Stuffed Cabbage

serves 10 to 12

Ingredients

- 1 large head green cabbage (look for big, smooth leaves)
- 1½ lbs. lean ground beef
- 1 medium onion, finely chopped
- 1 cup white rice, uncooked
- 2 cloves garlic, chopped
- 1 tsp. salt
- 1 tsp. pepper
- 2 (10.75-oz.) cans condensed tomato soup
- 2 (14.5-oz.) cans stewed tomatoes
- ¼ cup fresh basil, roughly chopped (optional)

Directions

Place cabbage stem-side down in pot with enough water to cover bottom half of cabbage. Bring to slow boil. Simmer cabbage for 10 to 15 minutes to soften leaves near stem. As leaves become softer and more pliable, cut from stem and set aside. When large- and medium-sized leaves have been removed, set remaining cabbage and stalk aside. Reserve about 3 cups cabbage water.

In a medium saucepan over medium heat, combine ground beef with onion, rice, garlic, salt, and pepper, and stir until browned.

Paula Broberg

Fall

To make cabbage rolls:

Using a sharp paring knife, slice a narrow strip, ¾- to 1-inch wide, from the thicker, vertical stem portion of the leaf. The goal is to reduce the thickness of the stem area on the leaf. Add 2-3 Tbsp. of beef mixture to base of leaf. Make one or two "rolls" around the beef. Fold over about ⅓ of one side of the remaining leaf around the beef mixture and continue rolling. Take the loose end of the roll (the one not tucked in) and, using your finger, push it into the roll, securing it. Place roll in pan used to simmer cabbage. Repeat until all the large and medium leaves have been rolled and placed into pan.

Pour tomato soup and stewed tomatoes over rolls and add reserved cabbage water to pan. Gently nudge cabbage rolls to allow soup mixture to cover in and around the rolls. Add extra cabbage pieces that were too small for rolling to pan. Sprinkle fresh basil on top of mixture. Bring liquid to a low simmer, and cook for 1 hour, checking at least once to make sure the liquid is covering the cabbage rolls. Add more salt if desired.

Vegetable Beef Soup

Ingredients

- 1 to 2 lbs. prime rib bones
- 4 (14-oz.) cans beef broth
- 2 cubes beef bouillon
- 1 large onion, diced
- 1 cup celery, chopped
- 1 cup carrots, chopped
- 2 (14.5-oz.) cans diced tomatoes
- 1 (14.5-oz.) can green beans, drained
- 1 cup frozen white corn
- 1 cup cabbage, shredded
- 2 tsp. ground parsley
- Salt and pepper to taste
- 2 small potatoes, diced
- 2 cups water

Directions

In a large stockpot, cook prime rib bones in water until meat is tender. Remove bones and set aside. Into same stockpot, add remaining ingredients. Bring soup to a rolling boil. Reduce heat and simmer, uncovered, for 30 minutes or until potatoes are tender, stirring frequently. Serve in hot bowls with rolls or French bread.

Turkey Noodle Soup

Finding new ways to use up all the leftover Thanksgiving turkey is sometimes a problem. Try my solution to this dilemma—a big pot of delicious turkey noodle soup.

Ingredients

- 1 turkey carcass
- 5 quarts water
- 1½ cups chopped celery, including leaves
- 1 cup chopped onion
- 7 chicken bouillon cubes
- 1 Tbsp. salt
- ¼ tsp. black pepper

- 1 bay leaf
- ½ cup chopped parsley
- 1 cup frozen peas
- 8 oz. fettuccine noodles
- ¼ cup (½ cube) butter
- ½ cup all-purpose flour

Directions

In an 8-quart heavy bottomed kettle, place turkey carcass, water, celery stalks and leaves, onion, bouillon cubes, salt, pepper, and bay leaf and bring to a boil. Reduce heat, and simmer, covered, for 1 hour. Remove carcass and let cool. Add parsley and peas to soup and return to a boil. Reduce heat and simmer for 10 minutes until peas are tender.

Remove meat from carcass, return pieces to soup, and discard bones. Return soup to a boil, add fettuccine, and cook, uncovered, for about 10 minutes. Melt butter in small frying pan, stir in flour, and cook over low heat, stirring constantly until flour is light brown, and add to boiling soup. Reduce heat and simmer another 5 minutes. Serve in hot bowls.

Fall

Old-fashioned Chicken and Noodles

There is nothing like a good bowl of chicken soup to take you back to the comforts of home. It's so satisfying, and it warms the tummy like nothing else can!

Ingredients

- 1 whole chicken, cut into pieces
- 5 cups water
- 2 cups chopped celery
- ½ cup chopped celery leaves
- 1 onion, diced
- 2 cups baby carrots, cut into thirds
- ½ cup fresh parsley, chopped
- 2 to 3 chicken bouillon cubes
- Fresh ground pepper to taste
- 8 oz. fettuccine noodles

"One of the best gifts you can give a friend is something you made yourself."

Directions

Place chicken pieces in a large stockpot, add enough water to cover chicken, and cook, covered, over medium heat until tender. Remove chicken from broth and set aside. Add celery, celery leaves, onion, carrots, parsley, chicken bouillon cubes to remaining chicken water. Add pepper to taste. Cook over medium heat until vegetables are tender. Add noodles and continue cooking until noodles are done. Add chicken pieces back to soup. This is delicious served in a bowl with mashed potatoes (see page 73) on the side.

Paula Broberg

Turkey and Cranberry Sandwich

Ingredients

- 1 loaf sourdough bread, sliced
- 1 (8-oz.) carton whipped cream cheese
- 2 lbs. turkey, sliced
- 1 (8-oz.) block Monterey jack or Muenster cheese, sliced
- 1 (14-oz.) can cranberry sauce, sliced thin

Directions

Arrange bread slices on a clean surface. Spread each slice with cream cheese. On half of bread slices, layer a slice of turkey, cheese, and cranberry sauce. Top each sandwich with another slice of bread. Cut into triangles and serve. These sandwiches are delicious paired with any of the homemade soups in this book.

chicken and noodles

Chicken Tetrazzini

This dish can be made with chicken or turkey. It's delicious either way.

Ingredients

- 4 bone-in chicken breasts
- 4 cups spaghetti or vermicelli
- 6 Tbsp. butter
- 1 cup fresh mushrooms, sliced
- ½ onion, chopped
- ½ cup chopped celery
- ¼ cup milk
- 1 cup sour cream
- 2 (10.75-oz.) cans cream of chicken soup
- 4-inch chunk Velveeta cheese, cubed
- ½ cup bread crumbs, canned or fresh
- ½ cup grated Parmesan cheese

Directions

Preheat oven to 350 degrees.

In a large saucepan, add enough water to cover chicken breasts. Cook chicken over medium heat until cooked through, about 1 hour. Remove chicken from heat, remove skin and bones, and cut into chunks. Set aside. Boil pasta in leftover broth according to directions on package.

In a separate skillet, melt butter and cook fresh mushrooms, onion, and celery until tender. Set aside.

In a large bowl, combine milk, sour cream, and chicken soup until mixed well. Add chicken pieces and mushroom mixture to sour cream mixture. Stir well to blend together. Add pasta and cubed Velveeta to bowl and continue to mix. Pour into a 9x12-inch baking dish. Sprinkle bread crumbs and Parmesan over top. Cover with foil and bake until cheese melts and dish is hot and bubbly, 45 to 60 minutes.

Paula Broberg

Fall

Paula's Chicken Pot Pie

This is one of those good, old-fashion comfort foods that provides a very satisfying main dish. This can also be made with turkey.

Ingredients

- 2 sheets frozen puffed pastry
- 4 bone-in chicken breasts
- 1 cup minced onions
- ½ cup celery, sliced small
- 3 Tbsp. + ¼ cup butter
- 1 cup sliced carrots
- 1 cup diced potatoes
- 1 cup chicken broth
- 1 cup frozen petite peas, cooked
- 4 Tbsp. flour
- 3 oz. cream cheese, softened
- ½ cup half and half
- ½ cup milk
- Salt and pepper to taste
- 1 egg, beaten

Directions

Preheat oven to 400 degrees.

Place the frozen pastry on a clean dry surface to thaw before unfolding. In a large saucepan, add enough water to cover chicken breasts. Cook chicken over medium heat until cooked through, approximately 1 hour. Remove chicken from heat, remove skin and bones, and cut into chunks. In a small skillet, sauté onion and celery in 3 tablespoons butter until tender, and set aside in a small bowl.

In a medium saucepan, cook carrots and potatoes in broth until tender, then add peas and cook an additional 5 minutes. Drain vegetables, reserving broth. In a large bowl, combine carrots, potatoes, peas, onions, celery, and chicken pieces.

In a small saucepan over medium-low heat, melt ¼ cup butter and slowly add flour, stirring until consistency is slightly thickened. Slowly add cream cheese and keep stirring. Add half-and-half, milk, and reserved chicken broth. Stir until creamy but not too thick. Pour cream cheese mixture over chicken and vegetables, and add salt and pepper to taste.

Fill 4 individual oven-proof bowls or ramekins with chicken mixture, then top with puffed pastry. Lightly brush pastry with beaten egg. Bake for 10 to 15 minutes, or until pastry is a rich, shiny, golden brown.

Fall

Mimi's Lasagna

Ingredients

- 1 lb. ground beef
- 1 onion, diced
- ½ bell pepper, chopped
- 5 cloves fresh garlic, diced
- 1½ cup sliced mushrooms
- 1 (14.5-oz.) can stewed tomatoes
- 2 (15-oz.) cans tomato sauce
- 1 tsp. marjoram
- ½ Tbsp. Italian seasoning
- ⅛ tsp. sugar
- ½ Tbsp. parsley
- Salt and pepper
- 1½ Tbsp. chopped black olives
- ¼ package spaghetti mix
- ½ box lasagna noodles, cooked as per directions
- 2 cups shredded mozzarella cheese
- 1 cup shredded mild cheddar cheese
- 2 cups shredded jack or provolone cheese
- 1 cup fresh grated Parmesan cheese

Directions

Preheat oven to 375 degrees.

In a large skillet, brown ground beef, onion, pepper, and garlic, and transfer to a large pot. Add mushrooms, stewed tomatoes, tomato sauce, spices, and olives to beef mixture. Simmer approximately 1 hour, add spaghetti mix into skillet, and cook an additional 15 minutes.

In the bottom of a 9x13-inch baking pan, pour 1½ cups meat sauce (or enough to cover the bottom of pan). Arrange a layer of cooked lasagna noodles evenly over sauce. Combine cheeses in a separate bowl. Sprinkle cheese mix over noodles. Repeat layering sauce, noodles, and cheese until lasagna reaches top of pan, ending with a layer of cheese. Bake lasagna for 45 minutes. Let stand for 10 minutes before serving.

Paula Broberg

Homemade Heaven Apple Dumplings

Ingredients

- 1 cup water
- 1 ¼ cups sugar, divided
- 2 Tbsp. flour
- 2 Tbsp. butter
- 2 Tbsp. lemon juice

- 1 tsp. vanilla
- 3 large cooking apples (tart apples, like Granny Smith, are best)
- ½ tsp. ground cinnamon
- 1 pie crust (see page 64)

Directions

Preheat oven to 350 degrees.

In a medium saucepan, combine water, 1 cup sugar, and flour, and bring to a boil. Cook until mixture starts to thicken. Add butter, lemon juice, and vanilla, stirring constantly. When butter is melted and sauce is mixed well, reduce heat and keep warm until ready to use.

Peel apples, cut in half, and scoop out cores. Set aside. In a small bowl, combine remaining sugar and cinnamon, and set aside.

Roll out pie crust and cut into 6-inch pastry squares. Place one apple half in the center of each pastry square and sprinkle a little of the cinnamon-sugar mixture over the top of each apple half. Moisten the corners of each pastry square and bring opposite points over the apple halves, being sure to overlap points and seal well.

Arrange dumplings in a 9x13-inch baking dish, leaving space between each dumpling. Pour hot syrup around dumplings. Bake for 30 minutes. Lift each dumpling into individual serving bowls, pour extra syrup around dumplings, and serve with ice cream. These are also delicious served warm by themselves.

Fall

Pumpkin Log

My granddaughter Christa made this for us one holiday. She got this recipe from her neighbor Joan. This is one of those wonderful additions to add to your autumn menu.

Ingredients

- ¾ cup flour
- 1 cup sugar
- 1 tsp. baking powder
- 2 tsp. cinnamon
- ½ tsp. salt
- 1 tsp. pumpkin pie spice
- ⅔ cup canned pumpkin
- 3 eggs, beaten
- 1 cup pecans, chopped
- 1 cup powdered sugar
- 8 oz. cream cheese, softened
- 6 Tbsp. butter, softened
- 1 tsp. vanilla

Directions

Preheat oven to 350 degrees.

In a large mixing bowl, sift together flour, sugar, baking powder, cinnamon, salt, and pumpkin pie spice. Add pumpkin and eggs, and beat until well blended. Line a cookie sheet with wax paper and spray with nonstick cooking spray. Pour pumpkin mixture onto wax paper and sprinkle pecans on top. Bake for 15 minutes. Remove from cookie sheet and allow to cool on wax paper.

While cake is cooling, mix together powdered sugar, cream cheese, butter, and vanilla in a small bowl. Once pumpkin cake has cooled, spread the filling over top. Starting on one end, carefully roll cake and transfer log onto a clean sheet of waxed paper and refrigerate until ready to serve.

To serve, place on a pretty dish and use a serrated knife for slicing.

Fall

Paula Broberg

Cranberry White Chocolate Chip Cookies

A treasure for the cookie jar! Everyone loves cookies, and everyone has a favorite. Chocolate chip, oatmeal, and brownies seem to be at the top of the list. This recipe is a version of my oatmeal raisin cookie, which has become a favorite during the holidays!

Ingredients

- ¾ cup sugar
- ¾ cup brown sugar
- ¾ cup butter, softened
- 2 eggs
- 2 Tbsp. flour
- 1 tsp. baking powder
- ½ tsp. cinnamon
- ¼ tsp. salt
- ⅓ cup milk
- 1 tsp. vanilla
- 3 cups rolled oats
- ¾ cup dried cranberries
- 1½ cups walnuts, chopped
- 1 cup white chocolate chips

Directions

Preheat oven to 350.

In a large bowl using an electric mixer, cream white sugar, brown sugar, and butter together. Beat in eggs. In a separate bowl, sift flour, baking powder, cinnamon, and salt.

To the wet mixture, alternate adding dry mixture with milk. After incorporating both dry ingredients and milk, stir in vanilla, oats, cranberries, nuts, and white chocolate chips.

Drop teaspoon-sized pieces of cookie dough onto cookie sheet and bake for 12 to 15 minutes, taking care to not overcook. Allow to cool on wax paper and store in a tightly sealed jar. Makes about 4 dozen.

Winter Season

"Reflecting on Seasons Past"

Winter is a time for soothing tummy warmers, those **comfort foods** we love so much on those cold and frosty nights at home. Here are some ideas to make your home more **cozy** and inviting. Keep a fire burning, put out a basket of fresh cranberries, bright red apples, lemons or oranges studded with cloves, pomegranates, nuts in their shells. Simmer potpourri with cinnamon sticks in it, **bake cookies** to munch on, or to fill the cookie jar for a later treat. There is nothing better than that sweet smell of bread baking in the oven. Then it's time for a good hot bowl of soup to warm the tummy.

Menu

Oatmeal with Maple Syrup

serves 4

Ingredients

- 2 cups water
- 5 cups Bob's Red Mill 5-grain oats
- 2 Tbsp. butter
- 4 bananas, sliced in half lengthwise
- 2 Tbsp. brown sugar
- 4 Tbsp. maple syrup
- 1 cup half-and-half
- 1 cup pecans, chopped

Directions

Bring water and oats to a boil in a medium saucepan over medium heat and cook until oats are tender, stirring frequently, usually 10 to 15 minutes.

Melt butter in a skillet over medium heat and add bananas. When bananas have lightly browned on one side, turn over and add brown sugar. Continue to cook until bananas are soft and caramelized. Divide oatmeal into bowls and top with maple syrup, half-and-half, caramelized bananas, and pecans.

Navy Bean Soup

Hearty bean soups are perfect starting in late fall, when the first chill comes on. There are a lot of different beans to choose from. Here is one of my favorites. This is the kind of soup that sticks to your ribs and is good for you too.

Ingredients

- 2 cups dry navy or great northern beans
- 5 cups organic chicken broth
- 1 ham hock
- 1 medium onion, chopped
- 1 stock celery, chopped (include leaves)
- 2 Tbsp. ketchup
- Fresh ground pepper and sea salt to taste

Directions

Rinse and sort beans in a large pot. Add 6 to 8 cups cold water and let stand for at least 6 to 8 hours (preferably overnight). Drain water and rinse beans. In the same pot, simmer broth, beans, ham, onion, and celery, and simmer for approximately 2 to 3 hours until beans are tender. Add ketchup, salt, and pepper to taste.

Serve in hot bowls. Corn bread seems to be just the right complement for any bean soup recipe.

Winter

Taco Soup

I enjoyed this soup at a birthday party given by my friends
Ed and Sandy; it is so easy to make and so delicious.

Ingredients

- 1½ lbs. ground beef
- 1 onion, chopped
- Salt and pepper to taste
- 1 packet taco seasoning mix
- 4 (14.5-oz.) cans stewed tomatoes
- 1 (14.75-oz.) can corn
- 1 (15-oz.) can black beans
- 1 (15-oz.) can white navy bean
- 1 (14.5-oz.) can green beans
- 1 (15-oz.) can garbanzo beans
- 1 (15-oz.) can pinto beans
- 1 (15-oz.) can kidney beans
- 2 (10-oz.) cans tomatoes with green chilies
- 1 packet dry ranch dressing mix
- 1 pint sour cream
- 1 bunch green onions, chopped
- 1 bag corn tortilla chips

Directions

Brown ground beef in a heavy-bottomed skillet over medium high heat. When meat is nearly done cooking, add onion, salt and pepper, taco seasoning mix, and set skillet aside. In a large soup pot, add tomatoes, corn, beans (including liquid), tomatoes and green chilies, and ranch mix. Add browned ground beef mixture into soup pot and stir well. Simmer over medium heat for 1 to 2 hours. Or, in a slow cooker, cook soup on low heat for 6 hours.

Serve soup in hot bowls and top with a tablespoon of sour cream and sprinkle green onions in each bowl. Eat with corn tortilla chips.

Winter

Paula Broberg

French Dip Sandwich

serves 4

Ingredients

- 1 packet au jus gravy mix
- 2 lbs. deli-sliced roast beef
- ¼ cup (½ cube) butter
- 1 onion, thinly sliced
- 1 lb. mushrooms, sliced
- 4 hoagie buns, split and warmed

Directions

In a saucepan, add au jus mix to roast beef according to packet directions. Simmer for 10 minutes to allow broth to cook into roast beef. In a separate small skillet, add butter, onion, and mushrooms and simmer until tender. Top a warm hoagie bun with roast beef, onions, and mushrooms. Serve with a cup of au jus for dipping.

Winter

Grandma's Classic Favorites for Holidays and Seasons

Beef Stew

Ingredients

- 2 Tbsp. olive oil
- 2 lbs. lean sirloin tip, cubed
- Flour for dusting
- ½ cup red wine
- 2 (14-oz.) cans beef broth
- 2 carrots, cut into 1-inch pieces
- 1 onion, chopped
- 2 stalks celery, cut into 1-inch pieces
- Kosher salt and fresh ground pepper to taste
- 2 medium potatoes, peeled and quartered
- 1 cup cabbage, shredded

Directions

Heat olive oil in a large cast iron skillet over medium heat. Lightly dust meat in flour and add to hot oil. Brown meat on all sides, add wine, and simmer, covered, for 5 to 10 minutes. Add beef broth and continue to simmer until beef is tender. Add carrots, onion, celery, and season with salt and pepper. When onions begin to turn translucent, add potatoes and cabbage. Continue cooking an additional 10 to 15 minutes until all vegetables are tender. Serve in hot bowls.

Karalynn's Stuffed Lasagna

This is a recipe from my niece. It is her family's favorite.

Ingredients

- 1 box extra large shell noodles
- 1½ lbs. ground turkey
- 2 Tbsp. olive oil
- ½ white onion, minced
- 1 Tbsp. Italian seasoning
- 1 tsp. garlic powder
- 1 jar pasta sauce
- 1 pint ricotta cheese
- 2 cups mozzarella cheese, grated
- ½ cup fresh Parmesan cheese, grated

Directions

Preheat oven to 350 degrees.

Cook shell pasta according to package directions. Drain and set shells aside. In a separate large skillet, brown ground turkey in olive oil. Add onion, Italian seasoning, garlic powder, half of sauce, and ricotta cheese to the turkey. Cook over medium heat. Remove from stove, then stuff the turkey mixture into cooked shells.

Arrange stuffed shells in a 9x13-inch deep baking dish. Pour remaining sauce over shells and sprinkle grated cheeses over the top, you may use as much as you like. Cover with foil and bake for 30 to 40 minutes till hot and bubbly. Serve with garlic bread.

Winter

Grandma's Classic Favorites for Holidays and Seasons

Merry's Peanut Butter Cookies

These are a sweet treat for the cookie jar, if you can keep any in there. My niece is an excellent cookie maker. Her family loves it when she comes to town, especially when she bakes up a batch of her mouth-watering cookies.

This recipe can be used to make a piecrust as well. Fill it with chocolate pudding for a scrumptious chocolate peanut butter pie.

Ingredients

- ¾ cup creamy peanut butter
- ½ cup shortening
- 1¼ cups brown sugar
- 1 box vanilla pudding
- 3 Tbsp. milk

- 1 Tbsp. vanilla
- 1 large egg
- 1¾ cups flour, sifted
- ¾ tsp. baking soda
- ¾ tsp. salt

Directions

Preheat oven to 375 degrees.

In a large mixing bowl, combine peanut butter, shortening, brown sugar, and pudding mix. Add milk, vanilla, and egg, beating until just blended. In a separate bowl, combine flour, baking soda, and salt, and sift together a couple of times. Add dry ingredients to peanut butter mixture and mix at low speed until blended.

Drop rounded teaspoons of cookie dough onto ungreased baking sheet. Flatten dough balls with fork in a crisscross pattern. Bake one sheet of cookies at a time for 7 to 8 minutes, or until set and just turning brown. Cool two minutes on baking sheet, then remove to wire rack to cool completely. Makes 3 dozen.

Paula Broberg

Snowball Cookies

This is one of my favorite cookie recipes. I think it may become your favorite too!

Ingredients

- ½ cup (1 cube) butter, softened
- 2 tsp. sugar
- 1 cup flour
- 1 tsp. vanilla
- 1 cup pecans, chopped
- Powdered sugar for rolling

Directions

Preheat oven to 300 degrees.

In a small bowl, mix butter and sugar till smooth and creamy, then add in flour and vanilla and mix well. Stir in chopped pecans. Shape into about 1-inch balls, then bake at for 30 minutes. Remove from oven then roll in powdered sugar while hot.

Winter

Popcorn Balls

This is always a favorite for children and adults alike. Chunky, munchy, and all together good.

Ingredients

- ½ cup (1 cube) butter
- 1 cup sugar
- ½ cup light corn syrup
- ½ tsp. salt
- 1 cup mini marshmallows
- 6 cups popped popcorn, spread out in cookie sheet

"A hot cup of cocoa and cookies shared with a friend on a cold winter day can warm and brighten up your world."

Directions

In a medium saucepan, combine butter and sugar. Cook over medium-low heat until sugar is dissolved. Add corn syrup and salt. Reduce heat to low and slowly add marshmallows, stirring constantly until mixture is smooth and creamy. Pour over cooked popcorn. Shape into balls. Allow popcorn balls to cool, then wrap in plastic wrap.

Winter

Paula Broberg

Index

Index

Grandma's Classic Favorites for Holidays and Seasons

Index

Grandma's Classic Favorites for Holidays and Seasons

Index

About the Author

Paula Broberg and her husband Ken owned a restaurant on the Oregon coast for many years. She currently lives in the beautiful Rogue Valley, surrounded by pine trees and mountains, where she receives inspiration from the changing of the seasons.

Paula has always loved cooking, entertaining, creating, and designing beautiful and interesting things. She enjoys writing poems and quotes, which you have found throughout the book.

0 26575 57939 0